RARE AIR

THE UNIVERSITY OF OREGON'S HISTORIC 2014 FOOTBALL SEASON

OREGONLIVE

The Oregonian

ON THE COVER (ABOVE): Marcus Mariota (8) makes a dramatic leap over Oregon State Beavers safety Justin Strong (39) at Reser Stadium during the Civil War. Bruce Ely/The Oregonian/OregonLive

LEFT: Thomas Tyner (24) and lineman Cameron Hunt (78) celebrate a touchdown vs. Stanford, Nov. 1, 2014. Tyner finished the season with 387 yards and three touchdowns on 88 carries and played in only nine of 13 regular-season games. Bruce Ely/The Oregonian/OregonLive

Published by Pediment Publishing, a division of The Pediment Group, Inc. www.pediment.com. Printed in Canada.

FOREWORD

Could even the most diehard Ducks fans see this coming?

A Pac 12 title. A Heisman Trophy. A Rose Bowl triumph. An appearance in the national championship game.

Rare Air, indeed.

You'd be forgiven if you hadn't predicted this considering how 2013 ended. The Ducks were excluded from the BCS for the first time in four years. That humbling disappointment bled into an offseason of turmoil. A veteran defensive coordinator was gone. Players were booted off the team for bad behavior. A star wide receiver blew out his knee.

Ducks fans knew they probably had the best college football player in the land. But surely Marcus Mariota couldn't do it all himself. Who would carry the ball? Who would catch it?

Even though the Ducks entered the season with a top five national ranking, they would take nothing for granted. When fall practice began, players were handed practice jerseys with blue collars – symbolizing the type of work ethic and attitude Mark Helfrich wanted to instill in his young team. That image of a hard-working, focused unit manifested itself each week. Aside from a home loss to Arizona, the Ducks met every test. With a hyper-drive offense and a scrappy defense, Oregon soared into the stratosphere. They avenged three straight losses to Stanford. They knocked off six nationally ranked teams. They annihilated the reigning national champs in the Rose Bowl, a team that hadn't lost in two years. Losing to Ohio State in the national championship game was tough to swallow. But it was an amazing season.

Whether he was passing, running or accepting awards, Mariota made fans proud. He became the first Duck ever to win the Heisman – and the first player from Oregon to claim the prize in more than 50 years. He did it with 4,454 passing yards, 770 rushing yards and that humble, hard-working selfless ethos that resonated with college football fans across the nation.

Mariota wasn't alone among Ducks standouts. When offensive lineman Jake Fisher returned from an injury to join center Hroniss Grasu, the Ducks line opened up gaping holes for freshman Royce Freeman, who rushed for 1,365 yards and scored 18 touchdowns. Freeman established himself as a future Heisman contender with his combination of speed and power running. All-American defensive back Ifo Ekpre-Olomu anchored a defense that was good enough to hold off the powerful offenses in the Pac-12. The Ducks overcame Ekpre-Olomu's season-ending injury and so many other setbacks. This team was resilient, determined.

The season was full of great plays, and one defining moment.

During a critical game against Utah, with the Ducks trailing, the Utes were inches away from extending their lead when wide receiver Kaelin Clay celebrated too soon on his way into the endzone. Clay dropped the ball just before he crossed the plane of the goal line.

Ducks linebacker Joe Walker picked up the ball and, with an escort of teammates, raced 100 yards for an Oregon touchdown.

Stunning. Unforgettable. Take nothing for granted.

We may not have seen any of this coming. But we enjoyed every minute of it.

— **MARK KATCHES**
EDITOR OF THE OREGONIAN AND OREGONLIVE

TABLE OF CONTENTS

[3]Oregon vs. South Dakota 7

[3]Oregon vs. [7]Michigan State...................13

[2]Oregon vs. Wyoming...........................23

[2]Oregon vs. Washington State...............29

[2]Oregon vs. Arizona............................35

[12]Oregon vs. [18]UCLA 45

[9]Oregon vs. Washington 55

[6]Oregon vs. California 61

[5]Oregon vs. Stanford 67

[4]Oregon vs. [17]Utah.................................77

[2]Oregon vs. Colorado 85

[2]Oregon vs. Oregon State 93

PAC 12 Championship...........................99

The Heisman 115

Rose Bowl 125

National Championship 141

Acknowledgements 160

LEFT: Marcus Mariota (8) won the Heisman Trophy, the first University of Oregon player to do so. He also won the Maxwell Award, the Walter Camp Award, the Davey O'Brien Award and the Johnny Unitas Golden Arm Award.

Randy L. Rasmussen/The Oregonian/OregonLive

#3 OREGON 62, SOUTH DAKOTA 13

OREGON OPENS SEASON WITH A FORESEEN ROUT

Oregon Ducks' changes bring a similar result: A season-opening rout of South Dakota

ANDREW GREIF
THE OREGONIAN/OREGONLIVE

EUGENE — The Oregon Ducks say they're always in search of change, and if there is any doubt of their intentions, they have the uniform combinations and roster turnover to prove it.

After an 11-2 debut in 2013 under head coach Mark Helfrich that didn't meet the Ducks' BCS-or-bust standards, change was welcome in Eugene in the nine-month offseason. It was most evident in the appointment of Don Pellum as defensive coordinator, and loss of UO's top four receivers.

But some things stay the same, too, and few could have left Autzen Stadium on Saturday night complaining about that.

OPPOSITE: Oregon stormed into Autzen Stadium for its season opener, then blew out South Dakota.
Michael Lloyd/The Oregonian/OregonLive

RIGHT: In his first game, freshman Royce Freeman runs for the second of his two touchdowns.
Randy L. Rasmussen/The Oregonian/OregonLive

Oregon rolled to yet another home-opening victory that echoed the best of its past while showing glimpses, brief but there, of some old concerns, too.

The opponent, South Dakota, was different as a first-time foe but the result, a 62-13 victory, felt as predictable as Oregon's nine previous home opening routs, a span in which UO has averaged 54.3 points.

South Dakota of the Football Championship Subdivision made Oregon uncomfortable in stretches, driving three times past Oregon's 31 in the first half by exploiting its lackluster open-field tackling and penalties, but the Coyotes inevitably became highlight fodder well before halftime.

The constant in Oregon's reloading is tempo, a 3-4 defense and Marcus Mariota, the junior quarterback who played just the first half but didn't need four quarters to justify his Heisman Trophy hype.

Surrounded by new faces at receiver and running back, Mariota passed for 267 yards and three touchdowns and ran for 43 more and a touchdown, becoming Oregon's career leader in touchdowns (82) in the process while tying Darron Thomas for UO's all-time touchdown passes (66). The Ducks gained 673 yards on 70 plays, with 32 first downs and one turnover. One important change was red-zone efficiency:

5-of-5 inside the 25-yard line, a stat that will make offensive coordinator Scott Frost smile.

"I'm just used to seeing that from Marcus," said Frost, who added one of Mariota's missed passes — trying to hit tight end Evan Baylis with receiver Keanon Lowe open over the middle — was his mistake for not getting the right players on the field. "It's great as a coordinator to call about anything and have Marcus make it work and I thought he did some really good things tonight but it's things we've seen all fall camp."

But strip away the names and you'd have had

trouble telling which vintage of Oregon football this was Saturday evening in front of a crowd of 57,338.

Oregon remains as fast as ever and fueled by the read-option running game that is as much the Ducks' trademark as a Nike swoosh. Royce Freeman is the newest flashy part in Oregon's machine and the true freshman running back scored twice — a one-yard dive and 26-yard run around the right side — on his first three touches. He finished with 75 yards on 10 carries and proved all the hype about his superb fall camp was real.

But it didn't provide much clarity into the real change of Oregon's season, a three-back rotation in which Thomas Tyner started Saturday and had 64 yards on 11 carries while Byron Marshall caught or rushed for 227 yards and two scores as he appears destined to replace De'Anthony Thomas as Oregon's multi-purpose offensive

nightmare.

On defense, Pellum rotated through two dozen players and the mixture suffered from the same bend-don't-break look that was the signature of his predecessor, Nick Aliotti — though South Dakota usually started with good field position due to inconsistent kickoff coverage, too.

Oregon allowed 5 yards per play while playing nearly double the amount of UO's offense, yet stuffed the Coyotes on two fourth downs, forced two fumbles (recovering one) and left them 7-of-17 on third downs, which was a weakness last season.

"No one, at least from the sideline … played great," Pellum said. "Just a lot of guys making plays but no one really stood out."

Pellum brought pressure from corner, running All-American corner Ifo Ekpre-Olomu — who would leave in the second quarter with an ankle injury — off the edge twice in the first quarter.

ABOVE LEFT: Byron Marshall runs from South Dakota defenders in the second quarter on an 11 yard pass from Marcus Mariota for his second touchdown of the day. Marshall's eight receptions, 138 yards gained, and two touchdowns were all high marks for his season. Michael Lloyd/The Oregonian/OregonLive

ABOVE RIGHT: With 14 seconds left in the first half, Marcus Mariota runs for a touchdown, his first rushing TD of the season. Randy L. Rasmussen/The Oregonian/OregonLive

OPPOSITE: Charles Nelson (6) and defensive back Reggie Daniels celebrate Nelson's 50-yard punt return for a third-quarter touchdown. Nelson would return another punt for a touchdown later in the season. Randy L. Rasmussen/The Oregonian/OregonLive

"I just tried to warm up on the field and coach (John) Neal said he didn't need me," Ekpre-Olomu said. "I'll be fine."

Oregon looked dashing as ever while still playing a vanilla scheme.

Whether this is change to truly believe in will be known next week when No. 8 Michigan State, of the same bruising style as Duck-wrecker Stanford, arrives in Autzen. ■

ABOVE RIGHT: Offensive lineman Matt Pierson (62) congratulates Kenny Bassett (31) on his 9-yard touchdown run in the fourth quarter, which capped the night's scoring. Randy L. Rasmussen/The Oregonian/OregonLive

BELOW RIGHT: Marcus Mariota (8) joins teammates in prayer on the Autzen Stadium turf following the game. Randy L. Rasmussen/The Oregonian/OregonLive

OPPOSITE: Players gather around head coach Mark Helfrich. Michael Lloyd/The Oregonian/OregonLive

BELOW: His night's work completed, Mariota spent the second half of the game on the sidelines. Michael Lloyd/The Oregonian/OregonLive

#3 OREGON 46, #7 MICHIGAN STATE 27

DECKED DUCKS BOUNCE BACK UP, SAVE SEASON

No. 3 Oregon Ducks show their College Football Playoff hopes are for real by beating No. 7 Michigan State, 46-27

ANDREW GREIF
THE OREGONIAN/OREGONLIVE

EUGENE — Punch Oregon in its mouth, past experience showed, and you could watch it stumble and fall, its once fleet green feet caught under the weight of linemen and expectations one and the same.

That perception that Oregon couldn't play against physical teams led head coach Mark Helfrich — whose Ducks were mauled in two losses in his debut last season — to remark sarcastically this week that, "If we lose to Stanford we need to blow everything up and start over."

Yet here were the No. 3 Ducks, after a showdown with No. 7 Michigan State that felt like a College Football Playoff semifinal in September, not only still standing but sprinting out of their Autzen Stadium tunnel and howling all the way

after escaping with a 46-27 victory.

The score doesn't indicate UO's struggle.

At one point in the third quarter, Oregon gained four combined yards on five consecutive drives as MSU quarterback Connor Cook shot holes through UO's secondary. He finished with 343 yards and two touchdowns.

But the Ducks didn't implode. Instead, they took two sticks of dynamite to the narrative they can't win a bar brawl by standing up to, and eventually sprinting away from, a Spartans team whose nine-point third quarter lead pushed Oregon to its brink.

"I was talking to Mark before the game and we

OPPOSITE: Michigan State's RJ Williamson gets a handful of Devon Allen's jersey but not much else as the Oregon receiver escapes for a 70-yard touchdown on a pass from Marcus Mariota. Thomas Boyd/The Oregonian/OregonLive

RIGHT: On a sweltering 91-degree day at Autzen Stadium, the Ducks came out of the tunnel in yellow.

Thomas Boyd/The Oregonian/OregonLive

figured if we lost the game they'd be saying Mark Helfrich is no Chip Kelly, and if (MSU) lost the game then the Big Ten isn't ready to compete with the power conferences," offensive coordinator Scott Frost said.

"That's all a bunch of hooey."

Oregon (2-0) stumbled but kept its footing, and now is sprinting at the head of the pack for the playoff chase.

Quarterback Marcus Mariota accounted for 360 of Oregon's 491 yards, passing for three touchdowns and converting key third-quarter third downs — after being 1-of-9 up to that point — that led UO to a 32-27 lead, one they would never look back from. On one he dodged pressure to pitch a desperation pass to Royce Freeman to get out of third-and-11. On the next drive he outsprinted four defenders to the first-down chain for 11 more yards before hitting Keanon Lowe four plays later for a 37-yard touchdown, a five-point lead and a giant Autzen exhale.

"I should pay to have to watch that guy play,"

Helfrich said.

Added Frost: "I told Marcus Mariota before the game this is what he was born for. I think he's the best football player in the country."

Any final judgment about Mariota must wait longer than two weeks, of course, just as Oregon's own worthiness won't be known until after its rugged nine-game Pac-12 schedule. But Saturday served as a tantalizing preview of the heights UO might reach.

Redshirt freshman receiver Devon Allen caught three passes for 110 yards and two went for crucial touchdowns. His 24-yard strike into the end zone's back right corner pulled UO within 27-25 and stalled the Spartans' 20-0 scoring run.

Oregon's defense, which but for a first-quarter interception by Erick Dargan had been shredded up the middle on both runs and pass alike for 24 points in the second quarter — its most points allowed in a quarter since 2008 — stiffened. Reserve inside linebacker Joe Walker started and

had nine tackles, two for losses, and helped UO with a key third-quarter stand.

"Michigan State is a physical team but we put our pants on the same," Dargan said. "... We just keep coming. ... I think we shell-shocked them a little bit."

In the fourth quarter, Ifo Ekpre-Olomu's diving

ABOVE LEFT: Erick Dargan's interception of Michigan State quarterback Connor Cook and 36-yard return set up Oregon's first scoring drive of the game.
Randy L. Rasmussen/The Oregonian/OregonLive

ABOVE RIGHT: Michigan State's Jeremy Langford (33) stiff-arms Dargan en route to a 16-yard run for the Spartans' first touchdown. Randy L. Rasmussen/The Oregonian/OregonLive

OPPOSITE: Dargan's interception led to a 1-yard touchdown run by Thomas Tyner (24) late in the first quarter that opened the scoring.
Thomas Boyd/The Oregonian/OregonLive

interception off a tipped ball and Royce Freeman's two touchdowns sealed Oregon's victory.

"I thought (Michigan State) thought this game was going to be a wipeout and I think they changed their demeanor," secondary coach John Neal said. "When things changed so quickly it was hard to get back."

And when the game shifted underneath both teams' feet Saturday, it was Oregon that remained standing. ∎

ABOVE RIGHT: Devon Allen celebrates his 70-yard touchdown reception from Mariota in the second quarter, the first of two Allen touchdowns for the afternoon. Thomas Boyd/The Oregonian/OregonLive

BELOW NEAR RIGHT: Allen was Mariota's target again in the third quarter, this time for a 24-yard score that got the Ducks within two points of Michigan State at 27-25. Randy L. Rasmussen/The Oregonian/OregonLive

BELOW FAR RIGHT: Wide receiver Keanon Lowe caught three passes for 58 yards in the game and scored his first touchdown of the season. Randy L. Rasmussen/The Oregonian/OregonLive

OPPOSITE: Lowe outruns the Michigan State secondary to complete a 37-yard touchdown pass from Mariota in the third quarter that put Oregon ahead for good. Thomas Boyd/The Oregonian/OregonLive

ABOVE: Oregon freshman Royce Freeman brought the home crowd to its feet with two fourth-quarter touchdown runs.

Thomas Boyd/The Oregonian/OregonLive

RIGHT: Freeman rushed for only 89 yards in the game, but his second fourth-quarter touchdown had the Ducks walking on air.

Thomas Boyd/The Oregonian/OregonLive

End of an era? Nope. Marcus Mariota saves Oregon's season

John Canzano
The Oregonian/OregonLive

EUGENE — Ron Mason is 65 years old. He makes $9.50 an hour working sideline security duty during Oregon football games at Autzen Stadium. When he reported for work on Saturday for the Michigan State game, Mason was assigned the visiting-team sideline and given explicit instructions should he encounter joyful Ducks fans leaping over the railing to rush the field after the game.

Said Mason: "We were told to let 'em go. And I'm too old for anything else."

No. 3 Oregon beat No. 7 Michigan State 46-27. Mason and his crew tried to "let 'em go." But in the end, nobody came. Very few Ducks fans hopped the railing. Almost none, in fact. It was as if Oregon's fan base had been here before, and expected to win, and acted like it.

Two quarters earlier, a funeral was being held for the era.

Oregon was done, right? They'd surrendered 24 second-quarter points to Michigan State. They'd fallen into a coma on offense. Gone was the edge. Lost was the identity. Marcus Mariota's final season was bleeding out in a 20-minute, 39-second scoreless span in which the Ducks played with the energy of a slug.

The Ducks had 14 rushing yards on offense in the first half. This means if you got off the couch and walked 59 feet during the intermission, and your dog got up and followed you, you'd both outgained them.

Oregon's season was going to be a goner. Dead. Over. Both coaches spent the week politicking for the college football playoff-selection committee. Lots of talk about how the loser would still have a chance to be in the final four. But the performance for a while was so anemic the entire season was slipping away.

"People around here are used to us getting yards easy and scoring easy," offensive coordinator Scott Frost said. "It can be frustrating (to call the game) when we're sputtering. We need those tempo plays. We knew we had to keep going

fast."

The Ducks started going fast. The rhythm picked up. The tempo returned. Oregon's lifeless corpse jumped out of the coffin during the funeral procession, and ripped off 21 points in a five-minute span in the second half. This was sparked by Mariota's feet, arm, brain and improvisational work.

After the game, coach Mark Helfrich was asked what it is that causes Mariota to get it going.

His answer: "Genetics."

Game ball to Toa Mariota and his wife, Alana.

I don't know what happens to Oregon football

after Mariota departs. Right now, I don't care. Because as long as No. 8 is in uniform, as long as he is healthy, as long as the Ducks have time on the clock, Mariota has this thing right where he wants it.

He threw for 318 yards and three touchdowns, including a 70-yard bullet down the seam to track star Devon Allen. He finished with 42 rushing yards. But it was his dancing in the pocket, his spinning out of trouble, the burst into the left flat and the flip to teammate Royce Freeman that became the difference between a death spiral and a victory march.

"Michigan State had one of the best defenses in the country last season," Frost said. "They're going to be one of the best defenses again this season."

They were fast, and physical, and flew around the field like someone in their old neighborhood had stolen their bicycle. The Spartans are good. They may even compete for the Big Ten conference title. But their playoff hopes are dust. I hardly believe the selection committee will ever forget the sight of Mariota gobbling them up in the second half and spitting them out like sunflower seed shells on the Autzen carpet.

Oregon's era over?

Puh-leeze.

An awful loss became a 19-point victory. This was like watching Kentucky trail North Carolina or Kansas by 10 in an early-season NCAA basketball game, only to have them come out in the second half and win by 30. Helfrich joked that his halftime speech was, "Gettysburg Addressish."

I'm thinking if Abe Lincoln had a field general like Mariota, he'd have KO'ed the South a couple of months earlier.

The knock on Oregon is that the Ducks can't beat physical teams. The losses in recent seasons to LSU, Ohio State, Auburn and Stanford suggest it. Be sure, the selection committee was watching Oregon-Michigan State to see for themselves. I suspect after seeing Oregon hang 46 points on MSU, Condoleezza Rice went to sleep wondering if there's a defense in America that can hold the Ducks under 35.

"Just because we don't run two backs out there and two tight ends people think we can't play physical," Frost said.

The Ducks played more physical Saturday. But mostly, Mariota knocked the will out of MSU's sideline one big play at a time.

Maybe you talk about Oregon's 22-19 loss to Auburn in the January 2011 BCS title game as if it were the great missed opportunity for the program. The Tigers won on that last-second field goal. Or maybe you look at the one-loss 2001 Ducks team as the one that got away. They might have been the best team in football.

That's nonsense that will never be settled.

Because this season can still be settled. This is the opportunity. There is no more looking back, only ahead. Oregon has everything it needs to run the table and play in the national semifinal for the right to go to the national title game this season.

There will never be another opportunity set up quite like this. There will never be a team as complete. And most compelling of all — there will never be another Marcus Mariota at Oregon.

"I should pay to watch him play," Helfrich said. He will, one day. ■

#2 OREGON 48, WYOMING 14

SLOW START'S BEGINNING A TREND

Behind Marcus Mariota's magic,
No. 2 Oregon Ducks overcome slow start
to beat Wyoming, 48-14

ANDREW GREIF
THE OREGONIAN/OREGONLIVE

EUGENE — Blame it on first-game jitters, the pressure of a top-10 matchup or the early wakeup call of an 11 a.m. kickoff, but Oregon's uptempo attack has yet to reach full speed early in any of their first three games.

The program that likes to channel Ferrari — the car company's Italian leather adorns UO's football complex — has had a tendency to jump off the line like a loaner. So it remained Saturday when after one quarter Wyoming led the nation's No. 2-ranked team, 7-0, as 56,533 at Autzen Stadium wiped the sleep out of their eyes.

"We were a little sluggish early in every phase," head coach Mark Helfrich said. "Who

knows, maybe a bit of a hangover situation."

Then, as they always seem to do, the Ducks pulled away.

The No. 2 Ducks have yet to play a perfect game, but when pushed they've had the perfect answers. Saturday, behind human highlight Marcus Mariota, that meant scoring 41 unanswered points to blow past Wyoming, 48-14, and end their nonconference schedule battered but unbeaten.

"We're right where we want to be at 3-0," Helfrich said, "but nowhere near where we want to be for the long term."

OPPOSITE: As is customary at Autzen Stadium, Oregon's mascot leads the team onto the field from the back of a motorcycle. Thomas Boyd/The Oregonian/OregonLive

ABOVE RIGHT: Marcus Mariota passed for two touchdowns and rushed for two more. Thomas Boyd/The Oregonian/OregonLive

BELOW RIGHT: Thomas Tyner rushed for 58 yards and had two pass receptions against Wyoming.

Thomas Boyd/The Oregonian/OregonLive

After three weeks, it appears how far the Ducks (3-0) advance in this inaugural season of the College Football Playoff will hinge on the health of the offense, opportunism of the defense and its readiness to answer the bell from kickoff.

Like in its previous games, Oregon's glimpses of sky-high potential were mixed with flashes of the vulnerabilities that will follow it into Pac-12 play next week at Washington State.

The offensive line suffered its third potentially significant injury when senior left tackle Jake Fisher was carted off with an ice bag on his left knee after UO's first drive — which ended with a turnover on downs three yards short of a touchdown.

He was replaced by Matt Pierson of West Linn, which gave UO a walk-on and a true freshman in Tyrell Crosby as its tackles.

"I feel really good about Tyrell and really good about Pierson if he's the guy," offensive coordinator Scott Frost said. "I'm counting on getting Jake ... and Andre (Yruretagoyena) both back pretty soon."

Thanks to Mariota's 221 passing yards, 71 rushing yards and four total touchdowns order was restored when UO scored touchdowns on its next six drives. His day was done after a five-yard touchdown pass to former UO point guard-turned-receiver Johnathan Loyd with 9:59 remaining in the third quarter.

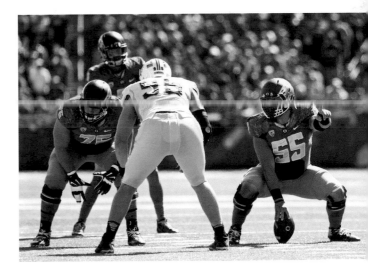

boys started 5-of-6 on third downs and gained 5.9 yards per play overall.

Most troubling was Oregon's susceptibility — whether the fault of one misaligned player or a larger issue — to long gains. The Ducks allowed four runs and six passes of 15 yards or longer. The Cowboys couldn't turn those plays into many points, but opponents like UCLA, Stanford and the like in Pac-12 play could.

"I'll be honest with you, in first half it wasn't what I wanted to see," defensive coordinator Don Pellum said of UO's push up front. "The biggest adjustment we made was to sit and talk about our tempo because we weren't playing hard and fast enough in my opinion. ... All of the sudden you could see us making some plays.

"That was the focus of my conversation at halftime; guys, we have to play faster."

And preferably earlier, too, though after another vintage Oregon finish, the Ducks are right where they want to be. ∎

Mariota provided the day's highlight on his second rushing touchdown, from 19 yards out, halfway through the second quarter that finished with Mariota diving from four yards out, over a blocking Duck receiver and his defender, and flipping head-over-heels past the pylon. If Mariota continues on his march to the school's first-ever Heisman Trophy, that moment — which put lumps in the throats of some of his coaches — will likely be replayed from Saturday until December.

"The coaches are always talking about when their defenders turn around they don't have their eyes on you," said Mariota, who reluctantly took advantage of poor coverage for many of his runs. "You can take off and that's what happened."

With two interceptions by safety Erick Dargan and a forced fumble by linebacker Torrodney Prevot, the Ducks' defense answered Wyoming's big plays with their own. The Cow-

LEFT: Mariota had plenty to smile about. The Ducks were 3-0 after beating Wyoming. His two touchdown passes in the game gave him 71 for his career in Eugene and at least one TD pass in all of his 29 starts.
Thomas Boyd/The Oregonian/OregonLive

OPPOSITE: Reserve receiver B.J. Kelley helped keep the Autzen Stadium crowd pumped up.
Thomas Boyd/The Oregonian/OregonLive

UO'S SHAKY DEFENSE, POROUS LINE OPEN UP QUESTIONS

No. 2 Oregon sidesteps Washington State's upset hopes but exposes big vulnerabilities in 38-31 win

ANDREW GREIF
THE OREGONIAN/OREGONLIVE

PULLMAN, Wash. — As a warm evening began on the Palouse, and as Oregon bounded through warm ups while top-ranked Florida State stumbled a few thousand miles away, the question arose: With a strong Pac-12 opener, could these Ducks ascend to No. 1?

After a barrage of big plays and blown assignments, it ended with No. 2 Oregon facing questions of a starkly different tone.

There are many, after a 38-31 victory against Washington State, but here is one: Does this team have what it takes — health and a sturdy defense, namely — to live up to expectations as a

legitimate College Football Playoff contender?

The answer to that will unfold in the coming weeks, but there is no doubt, however, that Oregon's bye week is arriving at the perfect time. Oregon's battered offensive line and oft-porous defense need to recuperate after allowing the

Cougars to rush past them to the tune of seven sacks and 499 total yards, respectively.

Marcus Mariota had never been sacked more than three times in a game in his career. After just two quarters Saturday, he'd been leveled five times, as weeks of concern about Oregon's

---

OPPOSITE: Marcus Mariota rushed for 58 net yards, a total that includes seven sacks by the Cougars' defense — five of them in the first half. Bruce Ely/The Oregonian/OregonLive

RIGHT: Mariota completed 21 of 25 passes for 329 yards and five touchdowns, two of them to Keanon Lowe, shown here celebrating with Mariota. Lowe had five catches for 104 yards, both season bests.

Bruce Ely/The Oregonian/OregonLive

injured line came to fruition. WSU finished with 11 tackles for loss.

"They were going after all of us," center Hroniss Grasu said. "They were just trying to do whatever it takes to collapse the pocket and they did a good job."

True freshman Tyrell Crosby started at left tackle, former walk-on Matt Pierson made his first start at right tackle, but the trouble extended to Oregon's veteran guards, too, who allowed a nine-yard sack of Mariota on the first series. It was a harbinger of an uncomfortable night for Oregon.

The line and defense never quite found their footing, as if the game were being played on one of the dozens of undulating wheat fields surrounding Martin Stadium.

How weird was this game?

Washington State, a team that regards its running backs as obligations rather than options, outgained Oregon's powerful rushing offense 28 to negative-12 after one quarter. And Ifo Ekpre-Olomu, regarded as one of the nation's best cornerbacks, was beaten on two Cougars passing touchdowns to start.

Washington State quarterback Connor Hal-

liday played superbly, completing 43-of-63 passes for 436 yards, four touchdowns and zero interceptions — his first INT-free game this season. His receivers took advantage of missed tackles by corner Dior Mathis and linebacker Torrodney Prevot on the opening drive that gave WSU a 7-0 lead on a 19-yard pass.

"They made some plays, there were some opportunities that we had and we actually got them in some longer yard situations and had a chance to get off the field and we didn't," defensive coordinator Don Pellum said.

Unfortunately for the upset-minded Cougars — who also couldn't overcome a missed 29-yard field goal, a fumbled punt return and two turnovers on downs — Mariota was excellent.

It was arguably his best performance of the season considering the pressure he found himself under and solidified his standing as the nation's best player at the moment.

Mariota completed 21-of-25 passes for 329 yards and five touchdowns and ran for his life amid

constant pressure, finishing with 58 yards on 13 rushes (most of which were scrambles to avoid another sack).

"There were four incompletions? Ridiculous. Ridiculous. That's a joke," Helfrich said. "That guy is special and he did a great job too of taking some of the blame and the heat off the o-line and led them through it and did a great job rallying

ABOVE: Mariota faced constant pressure from WSU's defense throughout the game. Bruce Ely/The Oregonian/OregonLive

RIGHT: Nobody could accuse Mariota of phoning it in against the Cougars. Despite enduring a rash of sacks, Oregon's star quarterback threw for 329 yards and five TDs. Bruce Ely/The Oregonian/OregonLive

OPPOSITE: With Washington State opting to wear white at home, the Ducks entered Pullman's Martin Stadium in black jerseys. Bruce Ely/The Oregonian/OregonLive

the defense in the second half, as well."

Even his misses were hard to knock, such as when he fought off a charging 299-pound Xavier Cooper in the red zone and somehow threw the ball away instead of taking a sack.

"I thought that was the play of the game," offensive coordinator Scott Frost said.

In the end, Florida State won in overtime in Tallahassee and Oregon pulled away, too, after nearly four hours of scratches from the Cougars' sharpened claws. They left deep marks and showed Oregon's vulnerability, just like another eye-opening road test from last season did, against Arizona.

The Ducks will face the Wildcats in a rematch on Thursday, Oct. 2, and it won't do so as No. 1. Oregon was No. 1 for seven weeks in 2010, and the last time was Nov. 11, 2012. A top ranking isn't required anymore in the College Football Playoff era, as the top four teams qualify.

"At first we started playing a little good here and there just glimpses and glimpses, but we have to finish and make sure the full picture is there," Prevot said.

After sidestepping a massive upset in the Palouse and exposing itself to hard questions,

whether Oregon can finish in the top four is up for debate.

"It was an ugly win," said safety Erick Dargan, who had a team-high 10 tackles. "But it was a win." ■

ABOVE LEFT: Facing an inspired Washington State defense, Mariota spent much of the night running for his life. Bruce Ely/The Oregonian/OregonLive

BELOW LEFT: Tony Washington (91) and Pharaoh Brown celebrate after Washington sacked Cougars quarterback Connor Halliday with 3:34 to play. It was Oregon's only sack of the night, but it was a big one. The Ducks sealed a difficult win by converting two first downs and running out the clock. Bruce Ely/The Oregonian/OregonLive

OPPOSITE TOP RIGHT: What offensive coordinator Scott Frost called "the play of the night" came when Mariota, knocked off balance in eluding WSU's onrushing Xavier Cooper, managed to throw the ball away and avoided yet another sack. Bruce Ely/The Oregonian/OregonLive

OPPOSITE TOP LEFT: Oregon's Byron Marshall reacts after his 15-yard run in the second quarter, which set up a Mariota touchdown pass to Devon Allen that gave the Ducks a 21-14 lead. Bruce Ely/The Oregonian/OregonLive

OPPOSITE BOTTOM RIGHT: Marshall had six pass receptions for 45 yards. Here, he eludes WSU's Sulaiman Hameed. Bruce Ely/The Oregonian/OregonLive

OPPOSITE BOTTOM LEFT: Hameed grabs Marshall's facemask in an attempt to slow down the Ducks' receiver. Oregon finished with 501 yards in offense. Bruce Ely/The Oregonian/OregonLive

WILDCATS HAVE DUCKS' NUMBER

Oregon Ducks now have a long weekend to fix what went wrong against Arizona in 31-24 loss

ANDREW GREIF
THE OREGONIAN/OREGONLIVE

EUGENE — Ten feet from a horde of reporters surrounding Oregon's defensive coordinator and a short jog from the field that the No. 2 Ducks had just stomped off, stunned after a home loss, John Neal sat back in a leather chair and stared ahead at a wall.

After Oregon's 31-24 loss to Arizona, the Ducks' secondary coach needed to take a seat for this one, and not only because he said he hadn't sat down in seven hours.

"You've got a lot of things on your mind right now and you think about we had a chance but we couldn't quite pull it off on some critical downs," Neal said. "We had third and long and they got it on a run play. It's tough. We had them stopped and we got a penalty. Stopped at least in terms of holding them to a field goal.

OPPOSITE: Running the football was tough for Marcus Mariota, who had a net one yard on nine carries.

Randy L. Rasmussen/The Oregonian/OregonLive

RIGHT: Oregon's Reggie Daniels (8) intercepted Arizona quarterback Anu Solomon in the first quarter, but the Ducks were forced to punt moments later.

Randy L. Rasmussen/The Oregonian/OregonLive

"And those things are going to be hard to live with when we really think about it and go, oh my goodness, what a way to lose."

Oregon has ample time for reflections like that after Thursday night's defeat, the earliest a Duck team has lost at home in conference play since Sept. 29, 2007, against Cal.

The plan all along was to use the two extra days on Friday and Saturday to prepare for what No. 8 UCLA does well, but now just as much time figures to be spent figuring out where Oregon (4-1, 1-1 Pac-12) went wrong, too.

Before Oregon's players and coaches filtered out of their football complex before midnight Thursday, they promised it will be time well spent.

"It's going to hurt, we'll digest it tomorrow," said senior inside linebacker Derrick Malone, whose 11 tackles tied for a team high. "It's going to hurt when we go over the film with coaches. When we start looking at the film of UCLA we've got to disregard that. We can't let one loss beat us twice."

What went wrong was a combination of 10 penalties, two fumbles, 13 allowed first downs and 21 points in the third quarter alone and injuries, too.

Oregon now has a jump on trying to correct them.

Junior defensive lineman Arik Armstead, who has been projected as a possible NFL first-round pick next spring, left late in the first half with ice around his left foot and ankle, limping into the locker room. He didn't return. Junior quarterback Marcus Mariota was not 100 percent, offensive coordinator Scott Frost said afterward, after being "banged up" from seven sacks on Sept. 20 at Washington State.

The undisclosed nicks and dings to Mariota might be one reason why Frost didn't roll him out, away from pressure, nearly as often as against Washington State, when the roll-outs were a crucial second-half adjustment. Excluding his five sacks Thursday, Mariota ran four times for one yard.

He had 12 incompletions, with at least four owing to drops or "miscommunication errors," where receivers stopped their routes 20 yards from where Mariota's pass landed. Mariota remains without an interception this season, but

at least two of his passes Thursday could have been the first.

"Hats off to them, they did a good job covering guys and getting pressure," Mariota said. "It happens but we have to execute better. ... It's obviously a testament to our conference, if you're not prepared each week or ready to play you'll lose."

Even if he wasn't full-go, Mariota should have had the ball on crucial plays more often, Frost said afterward in a self-critique.

Trailing 24-14 to start the fourth quarter, Oregon had first and goal, two yards from the end zone. It handed off on three consecutive run plays up the middle — Thomas Tyner for no gain, Royce Freeman for no gain, false start by guard Jake Pisarcik, and Freeman for three yards on third down. Oregon was 4-of-14 on third down. Oregon settled for a field goal.

Frost said each play contained multiple run-pass options.

"Like those third down calls, obviously I would call something else," Frost told reporters. "But those are the things we decide going into the game that are best going into those situations."

Often, though, play calls were moot because

the offensive line, while improved, still appeared too damaged from injuries to sustain protection either on runs or passes for as long as the Ducks needed.

Though Neal prefaced his comments by saying he needed to watch the film, he didn't need any video to know that two routes in particular killed Oregon's defense. They were wheel routes out of the backfield — a play Oregon's own offense has run for success several times this season with Byron Marshall — and Arizona turned them against UO.

A 54-yard route to Arizona running back Terris Jones-Grigsby up the right sideline got the ball to Oregon's 3 and set up a touchdown to give Arizona a 17-14 lead in the third quarter. Then, to check whether Oregon was sleeping, the Wildcats (5-0, 2-0) did it again on their next drive, this time for a 35-yard touchdown to Wilson down the left side.

"The two wheel routes were great calls," Neal said. "One of them we made a bad assignment and the other one we just, I'm not going to call it a missed assignment when there's someone not

covering a guy but it was a good throwback play and kind of tricked us a little bit. They got us. We're going to have to live with that."

One late stretch drew the deepest sigh from Neal, and will almost certainly be a talking point for Oregon moving forward.

With the game tied at 24-all in the fourth quarter, Arizona was pinned at Oregon's 33-yard line on third and 20, only to have running back Terris Jones-Grigsby break off a 24-yard rush.

Three plays later, Wildcat quarterback Anu Solomon was sacked on third-and-goal, creating fourth-and-17 — and then a flag was thrown. Unsportsmanlike conduct on defensive end

ABOVE: Byron Marshall (9) reacts to dropping a fourth down pass at the Arizona 31 on Oregon's first series. Arizona took over and drove to a field goal that gave the Wildcats an early lead. Thomas Boyd/The Oregonian/OregonLive

LEFT: Arizona's pass rush got to Mariota for five sacks over the course of the night.
Randy L. Rasmussen/The Oregonian/OregonLive

Tony Washington, who'd quickly bowed in a prayer pose after his sack. Four plays later, Jones-Grigsby ran in the go-ahead score.

"They deserved to win, too," Neal said. "I'm not going to say we deserved to win or we should have won or anything like that; I thought it was two even teams and two very similar teams and they were just one drive better than us.

"It's one great thing about being around this staff and Mark and we're not the kind of staff that, we're going to go beat our brains against the wall. We're going to pick each other up, shake each other's hands and say let's go get it back and see what happens. It's going to be a long year for a lot of teams and it's just beginning."

And for Oregon, a long weekend of figuring out what went wrong. ∎

TOP RIGHT: Royce Freeman led Oregon's rushing with 85 yards and also threw a 26-yard touchdown pass to Mariota on a trick play in the first quarter. Thomas Boyd/The Oregonian/OregonLive

BOTTOM RIGHT: This third-quarter touchdown catch by Devon Allen gave the Ducks a 14-10 lead. Randy L. Rasmussen/The Oregonian/OregonLive

BOTTOM LEFT: Freeman congratulates Allen after the latter's touchdown reception. Allen led the Ducks' receiving corps for the game with five receptions for 78 yards. Randy L. Rasmussen/The Oregonian/OregonLive

RIGHT: It was a night of bad breaks for the Ducks. Here linebacker Tyson Coleman returns an apparent fumble for an Oregon touchdown, only to have the play ruled dead before the ball came loose.

Thomas Boyd/The Oregonian/OregonLive

BELOW RIGHT: A key member of the Oregon defense and considered one of the best cover cornerbacks in the nation, Ifo Ekpre-Olomu got few chances against Arizona as the Wildcats rarely threw the ball in his direction.

Thomas Boyd/The Oregonian/OregonLive

OPPOSITE: Oregon Ducks wide receiver Devon Allen (5) catches a touchdown pass in the second half.

Thomas Boyd/The Oregonian/OregonLive

BELOW: Allen's longest pass reception of the night was a big one for the Ducks. In the fourth quarter, on fourth-and-11 from the Arizona 37, Mariota hit Allen for 28 yards to the Wildcats' 9-yard-line. Two plays later, Mariota threw to Keanon Lowe for the tying touchdown.

Thomas Boyd/The Oregonian/OregonLive

Heisman dreams in pieces, but Marcus Mariota remains whole

John Canzano
The Oregonian/OregonLive

EUGENE — On Thursday night, with his Heisman dreams lying in pieces on the Autzen Stadium carpet, and Oregon's perfect season demolished, Marcus Mariota did the most telling thing.

He stopped after Oregon's 31-24 loss to Arizona as he left the field and he approached a group of children. Then, he leaned over and shook their hands. The Ducks quarterback visited for a moment with a group of children who were at the game, on hiatus from a children's hospital.

With the third question in the postgame news conference, an Oregonian reporter asked a visibly disappointed Mariota about making that stop on the field.

"Those are kids," he said. "They wanted to come here and meet some of us, and meet some of the Ducks. It wouldn't hurt to just kind of talk to them a little bit, and get to know them. Win

or lose, that makes their day and that's all that matters."

Rewind one week. Because while Oregon enjoyed a bye last Saturday, there was no rest on the fourth floor of Randall Children's Hospital in Portland. It was here that 16-year-old Preston Miller fought for his life.

Miller has stage four Burkitt Lymphoma. He's hooked up to a half dozen IVs, dripping antibiotics and fluids into his blood. He's weak. He's lost half his body weight since summer. His skin is chafing so badly that it's cracked and infection

has set in. He'll require surgery on his skin. But doctors believe if they can get him strong enough, and build up his immune system, they can begin

---

ABOVE: Arizona took advantage of Oregon's injuries on the offensive line to score five sacks of Marcus Mariota.
Randy L. Rasmussen/The Oregonian/OregonLive

OPPOSITE: Oregon coach Mark Helfrich pleads his case to the officials during the Ducks' loss to Arizona.
Thomas Boyd/The Oregonian/OregonLive

chemotherapy, and might just be able to save his life.

"We're living this," said his father, David. "He's being kept alive by medicine. He's not even healthy enough to fight this right now. I'm not going to lie, I pray to God that if He's not going to help my son pull through this to not let him suffer so much."

Season in shambles? Everything ending? Tell that to the Millers, who wake up every day trying to hold their world together. Preston's father, who works for a logging company, spends weekends and nights at the hospital. His mother, Jaime, spends all day there, every day, along with family, including Preston's 9-year-old sister, Brooklyn.

Preston earned the nickname "MEV" at 6 months old. It stemmed from a visit to a restaurant, where he made a mess out of a bowl of rice.

"When he was in the room and healthy, he was the life of the room," his father said. "Big personality, big, big personality."

Last week, amid all the tubes and medicine and that bye week, the most interesting thing happened. A nurse walked in with a gift that had arrived courtesy of two Oregon football players. Hroniss Grasu, the Ducks' center, and Mariota, the Heisman frontrunner, had learned about Preston's fight.

They chipped in and bought a Mariota jersey together, signed it both. And sent it to the fourth floor, autographed with messages for Preston.

Wrote Mariota: "Get well soon!"

Wrote Grasu: "Keep fighting! Stay strong!"

RIGHT: Oregon Ducks tight end Pharaoh Brown (85) celebrates Devon Allen's touchdown catch in the third quarter. Thomas Boyd/The Oregonian/OregonLive

For the first time since July when his appendix ruptured, beginning what has become a heart-wrenching battle, Preston's cancer took a back seat to something else in the room.

"Cancer was secondary," his father said, "just for a second. The jersey was hanging on the wall. When he got it, it was like there wasn't any cancer for 10 minutes. He has no immune system, but he had that jersey and it made him think about something else for a spell."

There is no telling what happens to Oregon's football season. We don't know if the Ducks are a one-loss outfit that will make a playoff selection committee consider them again at the end of

the season or a program threatening to slip into obscurity. Uncertainty won the day on Thursday night, and it stuck around on Friday, just to make sure we all knew it.

But as I watched Mariota stop with those children, and later, talk about why it matters, I thought about Preston and the rest of the children on the fourth floor at Legacy Health's children's hospital. And I thought about Grasu and Mariota's quiet bye-week gesture.

Season spoiled? Heisman gone? Absolutely.

His father said: "Who does that? Who takes the time out of their day to help a kid who is fighting for his life?" ■

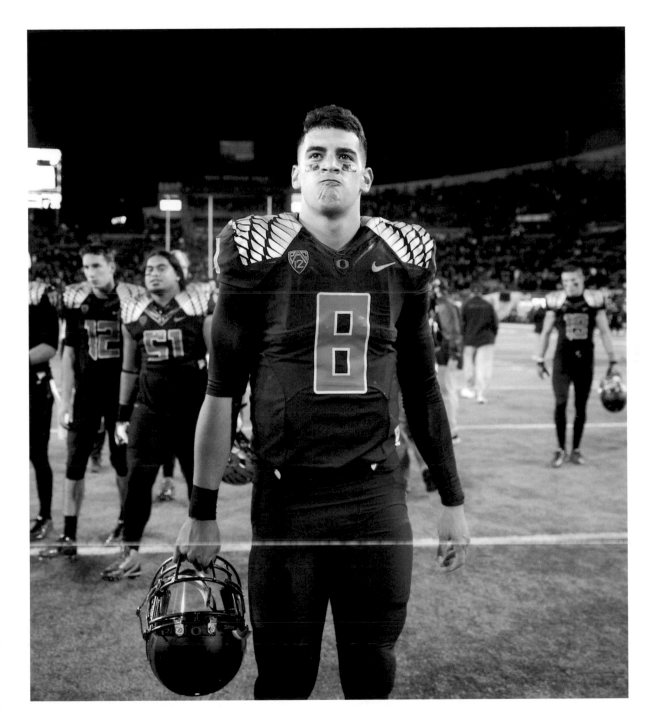

ABOVE: Arizona running back Terris Jones-Grigsby (on ground) is the center of his teammates' adulation after scoring the fourth-quarter touchdown that beat Oregon 31-24. Randy L. Rasmussen/The Oregonian/OregonLive

LEFT: A visibly dejected Mariota walks off the Autzen Stadium field. Despite his disappointment, Mariota took time to chat with children from a local hospital who attended the game. Randy L. Rasmussen/The Oregonian/OregonLive

BELOW: Helfrich, left, and his Ducks finally ran out of answers against Arizona.

Randy L. Rasmussen/The Oregonian/OregonLive

#12 OREGON 42, #18 UCLA 30

LOSING STREAK SNAPPED AT 1

Behind offensive line, No. 12 Oregon pushes No. 18 UCLA out of the way, and saves its season

ANDREW GREIF
THE OREGONIAN/OREGONLIVE

PASADENA, Calif. — It was four weeks ago when Oregon Ducks left tackle Jake Fisher left a game on the back of a cart, a bag of ice on his left knee and carrying his helmet.

After helping carry his team Saturday in the Rose Bowl, Fisher's exit took a slow, exultant route.

"We stuck it to them pretty well," Fisher said.

As the time ran down on No. 12 Oregon's 42-30 victory against No. 18 UCLA, he ran to a corner of the old stadium, where a wave of teammates in white and fans in yellow mixed in the shadow of the San Gabriel Mountains.

Before Fisher and the Ducks ran to their fans on Saturday, they ran for 258 yards over the Bruins in a victory that saved the season — at least for one more week.

En route to the locker room tunnel, 100 yards in the other direction, the din screaming Fisher's name approached a decibel level usually reserved only for quarterback Marcus Mariota. In one memorable yell, a fan professed her love to the left tackle.

Those aren't typical receptions for a senior of-fensive lineman, but then again the tenor around his team this week wasn't typical, either: Oregon, so beloved in polls and perception for so long, found itself battered by fans and media alike ever since a sloppy home loss to Arizona.

And one big concern was the offensive line, after allowing 12 sacks the past two games. ∎

OPPOSITE: On UCLA's second possession, the Ducks forced a fumble by Brett Hundley. Tony Washington (91) recovered for Oregon at the UCLA 13 yard line. Thomas Boyd/The Oregonian/OregonLive

RIGHT: On the very next snap, Oregon's Marcus Mariota dove for the pylon and came up with the Ducks' first touchdown. Thomas Boyd/The Oregonian/OregonLive

ABOVE: UCLA's Paul Perkins (24) rushed for 187 yards on 21 carries, but it wasn't enough as Oregon beat the Bruins for the sixth straight time.

Thomas Boyd/The Oregonian/OregonLive

RIGHT: With Jake Fisher (right) back in the lineup at left tackle, Mariota found time to pass for 210 yards and two touchdowns.

Thomas Boyd/The Oregonian/OregonLive

ABOVE: Oregon celebrates a third-quarter touchdown run by Royce Freeman (21) that made it 35-10. Freeman's 4-yard run was set up by Ifo Ekpre-Olamu's interception that gave Oregon the ball at the UCLA 10. Thomas Boyd/The Oregonian/OregonLive

LEFT: Just before Freeman's touchdown, Byron Marshall (9) carried the ball to the 4-yard line. Marshall also had five pass receptions for 41 yards. Thomas Boyd/The Oregonian/OregonLive

OPPOSITE: Oregon was not only good, but lucky. On one third-quarter play, Mariota recovered his own fumble and turned it into a 23-yard touchdown run, to the delight of his teammates. Thomas Boyd/The Oregonian/OregonLive

LEFT: Freshman Royce Freeman had what was becoming a typical day for the Ducks — 18 carries, 121 yards, two touchdowns.
Thomas Boyd/The Oregonian/OregonLive

FAR LEFT: Freeman was a handful for the UCLA defense. His 2-yard touchdown run early in the fourth quarter capped a 69-yard Oregon drive that put the Ducks up 42-10.
Thomas Boyd/The Oregonian/OregonLive

BELOW LEFT: UCLA's Jordan Payton, here in the grasp of the Ducks' Torrodney Prevot, caught both of quarterback Brett Hundley's touchdown passes.
Thomas Boyd/The Oregonian/OregonLive

BELOW: Oregon's defense made sure Freeman and the offense were never on the sidelines for long.
Thomas Boyd/The Oregonian/OregonLive

Ducks white-out past weeks' errors amid UCLA mess

JOHN CANZANO
THE OREGONIAN/OREGONLIVE

PASADENA, Calif. — This was a wedding, and whether you think they deserved it or not, the Oregon Ducks showed up dressed in white. Rose petals on the stadium grass. Guests seated in the sunshine, waiting. Cue the string quartet.

Oregon made Saturday afternoon feel that pretty again.

The Ducks beat UCLA 42-30, in a game that really wasn't that close. The squabbling this week came from the Bruins, who looked like a divided mess with coach Jim Mora Jr. in a spat on the sideline with his defensive coordinator, Jeff Ulbrich, in the second quarter.

UCLA was sloppy. Who invited them, anyway? The Bruins played undisciplined, raising a rifle and systematically shooting each of its toes off, one at a time, during the ceremony. But amid that distraction, Oregon looked like Oregon again.

"I thought we were loose," coach Mark Helfrich said. "I thought we were confident — and

for all the right reasons."

Ducks fans, you're forgiven if you had glassy eyes at the ceremony. This was like seeing an old friend you thought you might never see again walk the aisle. It's no guarantee that it lasts forever, or even shows up for another week. The fourth quarter was troubling, but after last week's debacle, this was a welcome sight.

Oregon was innovative and edgy again on offense. It challenged UCLA, one snap at a time. The Ducks were crisp, and played clean, and squeezed the Bruins into submission one gorgeous possession after another.

Run or pass?

UCLA didn't know, and it didn't apparently matter. Oregon executed as if it had never stopped looking wonderful. At one point, in the second half, the Ducks scored 14 points in 67 seconds. These were old times. During the scoring melee, quarterback Marcus Mariota tried to tuck the ball away and run a read-option, but fumbled it on the grass. Instead of jumping on the ball in a panic, as so many others might, he scooped it up like he'd dropped his car keys, and sprinted 23 yards for a score.

Rose Bowl attendance: 80,139.

You might argue that Saturday was about every fan who witnessed the dismantling of UCLA before their eyes. You might argue that it was about Oregon recapturing the kind of magic that had left the program in the last few weeks. You might argue that this was about Mariota interjecting himself back into the Heisman race and the Ducks trying to re-launch a campaign to maybe be included someday in the playoff.

You might also argue that one victory proved exactly nothing.

Those thoughts are all valid, and worth considering. But I'd argue that Saturday was primarily about one man before any of the other stuff — it was about Helfrich.

Chip Kelly, who had only seven losses in 53 games at Oregon, would never allow a freefall, would he? He would not permit a quiet slide into oblivion without a fight. When the Ducks lost under Kelly, they always responded with passion. After the loss in his awful career opener as head coach at Boise State in 2009 and a shaky win in

week two, Kelly's program ripped off six straight decisive victories. After Kelly lost to LSU in the season opener in 2011? Nine straight wins by Oregon, none closer than two touchdowns.

Was this Ducks staff in over his head? Would Oregon fall flat on its face? Was this the beginning of the end of the Ducks?

Kelly heard the criticism of Oregon from his new job in Philadelphia and sent a text message to offensive coordinator Scott Frost.

Kelly's text read: "Praise and blame is all the same."

The answer from Helfrich's Ducks came definitively and decisively, one beautiful snap at a time against UCLA. Oregon ran the ball. It strove to create, and maintain, tempo. Oh yes, this looked like old times.

This isn't to say that Helfrich's Ducks are back. Just that they appeared to have regained the shine and swagger that they lost in their last two outings. They looked formidable, and graceful, and edgy. The offensive line struggles are ongoing. And UCLA is a raving mess. But who cared on Saturday? Because Oregon made you wonder if they might just have their mojo back.

Actor Ty Burrell, on the sideline with the team, hugged Helfrich after the game. The man who plays Phil Dunphy on "Modern Family" told me, "Man, that's the Oregon we expect."

Booster Pat Kilkenny said from the sideline, "Mark needs a good night sleep ... and I think he just got one."

They sounded like wedding toasts.

Don Pellum's defense had looked vanilla before Saturday. That was half of Oregon's problem against Arizona. No adjustment on defense. No edge. But here they were against UCLA, active and flying around the stadium, putting pressure

on Hundley.

Oh, and absent was the post-play celebration nonsense that cost Oregon an unsportsmanlike conduct flag a week ago.

Second quarter, Oregon's Joe Walker shoots the A-gap and makes a big stop on a third-and-two play. UCLA had to settle for a field-goal attempt (41 yards, no good). After the stop, Walker hops up as if he's going to celebrate, looks to the Ducks sideline, then stops and just walks off.

Like he's been there before.

We waited for a response from Helfrich-led Oregon after a flat performance against Washington State. As an encore the Ducks got knocked out by Arizona. Oregon had itself to blame for being in this predicament. No free pass here. The Ducks failed to perform in consecutive weeks, and were exactly where they deserved to be. So there was no guarantee on Saturday. In fact, there was reasonable doubt that this program would ever walk tall again.

Nobody knew what to expect when Oregon emerged from the shadows of the tunnel at the Rose Bowl wearing those white uniforms.

The Ducks walked with that swagger again. May they hold onto it tighter this time. ∎

LEFT: On a sunny day in the Rose Bowl, Oregon coach Mark Helfrich got the Ducks out from under the clouds of their loss to Arizona. Thomas Boyd/The Oregonian/OregonLive

OPPOSITE: Marcus Mariota picked up both his team and his Heisman hopes on his 23-yard touchdown run after recovering his own fumble. Thomas Boyd/The Oregonian/OregonLive

AS ROYCE FREEMAN ROLLS, SO DO DUCKS

Turn it up to 11: Oregon Ducks crush Washington Huskies to continue rivalry dominance

ANDREW GREIF
THE OREGONIAN/OREGONLIVE

EUGENE — They looked like the Ducks of old Saturday night.

In image they looked like the 1994 version, donning retro uniforms of kelly green and bright yellow in tribute, and Kenny Wheaton retracing the 97-yard route of his program-altering interception on the back of a motorcycle before the game.

But in their play, a 45-20 victory against the Huskies at Autzen Stadium, the present-day Ducks instead resembled something closer to the grind-'em-up machine of the last decade that brought this program to prominence.

And just like those teams, these Ducks are

---

again crashing the national title discussion two weeks after being shown the door to the party, aided by Saturday's losses by No. 4 Baylor and No. 5 Notre Dame.

All the hallmarks were on display in front of 57,858. The Ducks produced a 100-yard rusher for a second consecutive game in Royce Freeman, and the freshman responded with four touchdowns. Oregon's opportunistic defense

also forced two turnovers against a Husky team with just one in its first six games. UW's first touchdown came on its eighth drive, midway through the third quarter.

"One of the goals was to get the ball and change the game," defensive coordinator Don Pellum said, describing an interception by Erick Dargan and a forced fumble by Christian French. "Our kids took it to heart and took a couple

takeaways."

It all led to something else familiar, too: an 11th straight Oregon win against Washington.

The Ducks ran directly into the teeth of the defense and gouged 218 yards, on 4.4 yards per carry. Nearly four weeks after its seven sacks allowed to Washington State marked an ebb in confidence, the line puffed out their collective chests afterward and described a game plan that wanted to fatigue Washington with repeated runs and tempo.

When left guard Hamani Stevens hopped off the field to get his right ankle re-taped in the first quarter, the Ducks scored three plays later on an option pitch from quarterback Marcus Mariota to Freeman by running to the left side, missing starter be damned.

"We're not going to change the way we run the ball because they're strong inside on their front seven," Grasu said. "We knew that going into the game and as an offensive line we took that as a challenge."

With 8:30 remaining in the first quarter, Freeman rushed untouched up the middle for a 37-yard touchdown, run sprung by center Hroniss Grasu's pancake block on star linebacker Shaq Thompson and Stevens' block on Danny Shelton, a mountain-sized defensive tackle.

It was the first of four touchdowns on the night by Freeman — a fifth was negated by a holding penalty — and his career-high 169 yards on 29 carries almost assuredly removes any further mystery about the pecking order in Oregon's backfield. Freeman's carries bookended Oregon's 99 ½-yard second-quarter touchdown drive to take a 21-6 lead.

It was symbolic that a freshman would take the game over, after Wheaton did the same two decades ago.

"When you can run the ball," head coach Mark Helfrich said, "you can do anything."

Offensive coordinator Scott Frost believes Freeman "turned a corner" and ran for the first time without hesitation last week against UCLA, and indeed he was full-speed ahead against the likes of defensive linemen Shelton and Hau'oli Kikaha, who each ranked nationally in the top-10 in tackles for loss and combined for five Saturday. Freeman's bruising style allowed the Ducks to score touchdowns on four of six drives into the red zone.

"You saw some of (Freeman's) elusiveness that was kind of legendary there in fall camp," Helfrich said. "He's a guy who can run through

LEFT: Freeman's 37-yard touchdown burst through the Huskies' defense in the first quarter was his longest run of the day and staked the Ducks to a 7-3 lead. They never trailed again. Bruce Ely/The Oregonian/OregonLive

OPPOSITE: While Freeman (left) often seemed a blur to Washington's run defense, Marcus Mariota shredded the Huskies' secondary for 336 yards passing and two touchdowns. Thomas Boyd/The Oregonian/OregonLive

guys and a guy who can make people miss a little better than you think. He's starting to play free of thought and letting his natural gifts take over."

His ascendance was contrasted by sophomore Thomas Tyner's disappearance due to an undisclosed injury that caused him to miss the final three quarters.

Frost described Tyner as "fine" but couldn't pinpoint when he'd been hurt. Tyner finished with three carries for one yard and a reception for 13.

Almost forgotten in the night was Mariota surpassing 10,000 career yards of total offense, and 8,000 career passing yards, becoming just the third Duck quarterback to ever reach that passing plateau.

"24-of-33, 336 (yards) and two (touchdowns) is OK, right?" Helfrich joked. ∎

ABOVE: Freshman receiver Darren Carrington caught five passes for 79 yards. Thomas Boyd/The Oregonian/OregonLive

ABOVE LEFT: Carrington (87) celebrates with Marshall after the latter's 23-yard touchdown reception put the Ducks up 28-6 at halftime. Thomas Boyd/The Oregonian/OregonLive

BELOW LEFT: Dwayne Stanford's spectacular touchdown catch in the left corner of the end zone caps Oregon's first drive of the second half.

Thomas Boyd/The Oregonian/OregonLive

OPPOSITE TOP RIGHT: Former Oregon players hoist ex-coach Rich Brooks during a timeout. Brooks coached the 1994 Ducks to the program's first appearance in the Rose Bowl game in 37 years. Bruce Ely/The Oregonian/OregonLive

OPPOSITE BOTTOM RIGHT: Erick Dargan's second-quarter interception gave the Ducks the ball at the Washington 23, from which Marcus Mariota hit Marshall with a touchdown pass two plays later.

Thomas Boyd/The Oregonian/OregonLive

OPPOSITE BOTTOM LEFT: Byron Marshall skips over UW's Sidney Jones. In addition to his touchdown reception, Marshall rushed five times for 30 yards.

Bruce Ely/The Oregonian/OregonLive

OPPOSITE TOP LEFT: Oregon's offensive line kept the Huskies' pass rush at bay. Bruce Ely/The Oregonian/OregonLive

#6 OREGON 59, CALIFORNIA 41

DUCKS MAKE THEIR PLAYOFF CASE

Oregon makes its case as the class of the Pac-12 with 59-41 win over Cal, but bigger questions remain

ANDREW GREIF
THE OREGONIAN/OREGONLIVE

SANTA CLARA, Calif. — Four days before the College Football Playoff's selection committee pulls back its curtain and unveils its first ranking, the Oregon Ducks presented a convincing case as the Pac-12's best team under Friday night's lights here.

Quickly, the points added up in a 59-41 victory against Cal. In a two-hour first half, the Bears and Ducks combined for 66 of them.

But after a night with peerless offense and murky defense, a question remains: When the committee's final four is announced Dec. 7, where will Oregon stack up?

With a third resounding victory in as many weeks the Ducks (7-1, 4-1 Pac-12) have positioned themselves as the class of their conference by

rolling up more than 500 yards on the not-so-Golden Bears (4-4, 2-4), losers of three straight. It was only three weeks ago that Cal was atop the Pac-12's North division, the beneficiaries of conference chaos.

Buoyed by better health and quarterback Marcus Mariota's unrelenting assault on the record books — he broke Bill Musgrave's all-time passing yardage record at Oregon on a 22-yard first-quarter touchdown to Dwayne

OPPOSITE: Oregon receiver Dwayne Stanford was Marcus Mariota's favorite target on this night. Stanford had six receptions for 103 yards and two touchdowns.

Randy L. Rasmussen/The Oregonian/OregonLive

RIGHT: Mariota left most of the running to others, finishing with just 36 yards on six carries.

Randy L. Rasmussen/The Oregonian/OregonLive

Stanford — the Ducks have retaken the mantle so many expected in the preseason. A return trip to Levi's Stadium, Friday's venue, for the Pac-12 championship game looks increasingly likely.

"Marcus is such a stud and it's great that he has another year and a half left," head coach Mark Helfrich said, drawing laughs from reporters. He followed in mock disbelief: "What?"

The Ducks improved to 62-2 since 2009 when scoring more than 30 points, and 18-0 under Helfrich after scoring on five of their first six drives and withstanding a wild end of the first half that put a lump in Ducks fans' throats.

After Mariota threw his first interception in 253 attempts with 1:56 remaining in the second quarter — safety Stefan McClure picked it in the end zone after two teammates batted it away — the Ducks dodged a bullet by forcing a suddenly empowered Bears team to punt up 31-28. But then UO's Ayele Forde was pushed into touching the punt, which gave the ball back to Cal 40 yards from the end zone and taking the

lead.

That is, before a rule review handed the ball back to Oregon.

It was the beginning of the end for Cal.

The Ducks coolly answered three plays and 60 yards later on a 24-yard pass from Mariota to Dwayne Stanford, one of his two receiving touchdowns.

Mariota, expected to be the No. 1 overall pick in the 2015 NFL draft, looked right at home in the home of the San Francisco 49ers by completing 18-of-30 passes for 326 yards and five touchdowns with an interception.

Oregon then scored on its first two drives of the second half to go up 52-28, including a back-breaker of a 54-yard pass to Byron Marshall on third-and-21, and all pretense of drama was lost. Freshman running back Royce Freeman rolled up his third consecutive 100-yard game and wore the resolve right out of Cal with every one of his bruising attempts.

Pharaoh Brown added two receiving touchdowns, giving him five this season, or three more scores than he had in all of 2013. Freshman special teams dynamo Charles Nelson had another signature game by scoring on a 58-yard punt return and jarring a fumble loose on Cal's punt coverage, too.

But it remains to be seen what three victories against opponents that appear more exposed by the week mean in the grand scheme. And also, whether an Oregon defensive performance that allowed nearly 600 yards to a young Cal squad was the exception to its recent run of encouraging performances or a regression to the mean.

"I think when it got to 31-14, a few of our guys took a deep breath and relaxed too much and that's on all of us collectively to have the killer

instinct mindset of finishing the deal," Helfrich said. "Against those guys you're not going to finish it in the first half, they're too talented. But after the punt return I think there was a bit too much of that."

It tightened in the second half, allowing just a touchdown, and forced key stops on fourth down and by a fumble, yet its first-half performance might give some — maybe the 12 selection committee members? — pause when answering where Oregon belongs amid the na-

ABOVE: Tight end Pharaoh Brown had an efficient night — two receptions, two touchdowns, including this 9-yard catch that gave Oregon a 10-point lead in the second quarter. Randy L. Rasmussen/The Oregonian/OregonLive

RIGHT: Mariota threw five touchdown passes, but also threw his first interception of 2014, breaking a streak of 253 pass attempts without a pick.
Randy L. Rasmussen/The Oregonian/OregonLive

tion's heavyweights if it has to win by shootout more often than not.

Here's the thing: That final answer isn't due for another six weeks.

"That's a really good football team," said Helfrich, acknowledging that just winning isn't enough with Oregon — winning with style is expected. "To win on the road, short week, a bunch of guys gutting it out, you know, you can't just look at numbers and say, these guys stink."

There's plenty of time for the four SEC teams ahead of Oregon to cannibalize themselves. And lots of time to wonder whether being the best in a Pac-12 with few true contenders will be enough to be considered among the best in the country. ■

TOP RIGHT: Charles Nelson's 58-yard punt return for a touchdown was his second trip to the end zone with a punt this season. Randy L. Rasmussen/The Oregonian/OregonLive

BOTTOM RIGHT: What was statistically Stanford's best game of the season came at the worst time for California. Randy L. Rasmussen/The Oregonian/OregonLive

LEFT: Byron Marshall gave another demonstration of his versatility. The Ducks' junior rushed seven times for 57 yards and caught four passes for 133 yards, including a 54-yard touchdown from Mariota that put Oregon up by 17 points early in the second half.
Randy L. Rasmussen/The Oregonian/OregonLive

ABOVE: It was a big night for Oregon receivers. Stanford celebrates with teammates after his 24-yard touchdown pass from Mariota — Stanford's second TD of the game — made it 38-28 just before halftime.

Randy L. Rasmussen/The Oregonian/OregonLive

ABOVE LEFT: Brown had touchdown catches of nine and 21 yards, respectively — the latter score slamming the door on California in the fourth quarter.

Randy L. Rasmussen/The Oregonian/OregonLive

BELOW LEFT: Marshall high-steps his way to the end zone at the end of a 54-yard pass-and-run play as Oregon repeatedly took advantage of Cal's young defense.

Randy L. Rasmussen/The Oregonian/OregonLive

OPPOSITE: Mariota hung loose at Levi's Stadium and accounted for 362 of Oregon's 590 yards of offense.

Randy L. Rasmussen/The Oregonian/OregonLive

#5 OREGON 45, STANFORD 16

STANFORD HAS A NASTY OREGON PROBLEM

A simple piece of paper fuels No. 5 Oregon's 45-16 win against Stanford

ANDREW GREIF
THE OREGONIAN/OREGONLIVE

EUGENE — No one can quite remember when the flyer appeared in Oregon's locker room this year.

Maybe it was after spring practice? Or during fall camp? Not that it matters much. Because no one forgot what it said.

"It had the ESPN people and what they said," freshman receiver Darren Carrington said Saturday after leaving a raucous locker room, a much different scene from the one when the paper showed up in the offseason earlier this year. "They said Oregon's too soft for Stanford."

Carrington grinned.

"Maybe," he said, "they have a change of opinion now?"

In the aftermath of No. 5 Oregon's 45-16 win against Stanford on Saturday, a win that snapped

UO's two-year losing streak to the Cardinal and buried the talk of a so-called "Stanford problem," change has come in many ways to the Pac-12 North, where the recent rivalry between the schools — polar opposites in style, scheme and branding — was the talk of the division.

The Ducks are now two games ahead of the Cardinal with three games to play. For the past two years, the North division went through Stanford. On Saturday night, though, it was Oregon that went through Stanford.

"It's a prideful group right now," said head coach Mark Helfrich, who joked about the losing streak, "Was there ever an actual monkey

---

OPPOSITE: Oregon defender Alex Balducci (56) gave Stanford's Remound Wright a painful lesson in running sideways. The Oregon defense held Stanford to 132 yards rushing on 39 attempts. Bruce Ely/The Oregonian/OregonLive

RIGHT: Marcus Mariota rushed for 669 yards on 117 carries for the season, scoring 14 touchdowns along the way. Bruce Ely/The Oregonian/OregonLive

on my back?"

"No, I think the issues that we had for the most part and again, this isn't to take anything away from Stanford, we had an Oregon problem," he said. "It was our individual issues here and there, team here and there, coaching here and there, that led to two losses. Obviously, very pleased about the result tonight."

It was a potentially costly win, with starting right tackle Matt Pierson suffering an injured MCL in his left knee — he could be out at least two weeks — and defensive lineman Arik Armstead appearing to reinjure a left ankle in the first half.

Oregon's 45 points and 525 yards were the most by a Stanford opponent since Oct. 6, 2012. Between that date and Saturday, opponents hadn't scored more than 30 points in 31 straight games, or piled up more than 400 yards in 15 straight games — both streaks led the nation.

That was until Saturday, when UO quarterback Marcus Mariota was far from his Heisman Trophy candidate self yet still passed for 258 yards (he also threw his second interception this season) and two touchdowns and ran for 85 yards and two more scores. He set the tone on the first drive, when on fourth-and-5 he eluded two sure-tackling Cardinal in the backfield for a 21-yard gain. The Ducks would go on to score, on a six-yard pass to speedy Charles Nelson.

"A play is never ended with Marcus back there," said Carrington, who caught a 26-yard touchdown from Mariota in his trademark toe-touch style. "You just know something's going to happen. He's like Houdini."

This season, no defense had been better than Stanford's, after it allowed an average of 250 yards per game. The Ducks (8-1, 5-1 Pac-12) had

312 at halftime.

"This year it was awesome to have the tides turn around a little bit," Mariota said.

Unlike past seasons when Stanford's ball-control offense magnified every Oregon mistake, the Ducks put the pressure on from the beginning. Stanford's defense allowed opponents 12.5 points per game. The Ducks had two touch-

downs in the first nine minutes. Meanwhile, Stanford settled for two field goals on as many drives.

Facing a fourth-and-4 from the Oregon 25 on its next drive, Stanford (5-4, 3-3) gambled and went for it, hoping a touchdown might create a spark. Instead, Oregon linebacker Derrick Malone tipped Kevin Hogan's pass, and Oregon

OPPOSITE: Usually a kick-return specialist, freshman Charles Nelson caught this 6-yard touchdown pass from Mariota on Oregon's first offensive series.
Thomas Boyd/The Oregonian/OregonLive

LEFT: Mariota's performance was tough for Stanford to handle. Mariota threw an interception — his second and last of the regular season — and two touchdown passes. The latter gave him at least one TD pass in every game he has started for the Ducks. Bruce Ely/The Oregonian/OregonLive

BOTTOM LEFT: Mariota's extraordinary running ability gives the Ducks' offense an additional dimension. Mariota ran for two touchdowns against Stanford.
Bruce Ely/The Oregonian/OregonLive

BOTTOM RIGHT: Eight different receivers caught passes for Oregon against Stanford, including three receptions by Dwayne, the Ducks' Stanford.
Thomas Boyd/The Oregonian/OregonLive

tacked on a field goal on its ensuing drive to take a 24-6 lead in the second quarter.

UO safety Erick Dargan, whose dozen tackles were a team high, would force Hogan into two more critical errors, the first an interception on an overthrown ball near the UO goal line (Dargan's fifth this season) and a forced fumble on a Hogan scramble that Tony Washington recovered.

"The kids took the challenge," said defensive coordinator Don Pellum, whose unit allowed its fewest points since Sept. 13. "The pad level was good, the gap control was good for the most part, I mean there were a couple plays, but overall they accepted the challenge and performed really well."

With 29 seconds left on the clock, defensive end DeForest Buckner tried to embrace Pellum,

whose defense had come under siege.

"I told him no, not yet," Pellum said. "Then, obviously, I gave him a big hug."

Two plays after Dargan's forced fumble, Mariota waltzed into the end zone for a seven-yard touchdown and 38-16 lead, helped by a crack-back block from receiver Nelson on a would-be tackler.

The defender never saw it coming.

Neither did many predict this result, not with the Cardinal's reputation as a defensive stalwart and holder of glowing Oregon kryptonite.

At least, outside of the Oregon locker room, where a piece of paper became a symbol of a nation's doubts.

"We took that as disrespectful," Fisher said of the "too soft" headline, adding that he believed the paper was a creation of UO graduate assistant Joe Bernardi.

Added Malone: "It's been there for a very, very long time."

It wasn't clear whether he was talking about the paper itself, or the perception that had stuck in the Ducks' beaks ever since last November,

---

OPPOSITE: Featured running back Royce Freeman rushed for a team-best 98 yards and added 52 yards on three pass receptions. Bruce Ely/The Oregonian/OregonLive

TOP LEFT: Wide receiver Dwayne Stanford gained 27 yards on three receptions for the game.
Bruce Ely/The Oregonian/OregonLive

BOTTOM LEFT: Crunch time for Stanford quarterback Kevin Hogan came on this second-quarter sack by Oregon's Christian French and Rodney Hardrick (behind French).
Thomas Boyd/The Oregonian/OregonLive

when the Cardinal knocked the Ducks' title hopes askew. Maybe it didn't matter.

"You can't forget," Malone said. "You've got to keep that fire." ∎

TOP RIGHT: Oregon linebackers French (96) and Hardrick (48) brought the pain to Stanford's Kevin Hogan.

Thomas Boyd/The Oregonian/OregonLive

BOTTOM RIGHT: The ball is loose after Erick Dargan (4) strips Hogan early in the fourth quarter. Oregon's Tony Washington recovered, setting up a Ducks touchdown.

Bruce Ely/The Oregonian/OregonLive

BOTTOM LEFT: Defensive lineman DeForest Bucker (44) and friends have plenty to smile about after limiting Stanford to just 132 yards rushing and allowing the Cardinal only six third-down conversions.

Thomas Boyd/The Oregonian/OregonLive

Mariota's ease with Stanford overrides last year's downer

JOHN CANZANO
THE OREGONIAN/OREGONLIVE

EUGENE — Early last November, in the minutes after Oregon's loss to the Cardinal, Toa Mariota, made his way through the tunnel at Stanford Stadium, found a shadow outside the door to the visiting locker room and waited for his son, Marcus.

Marcus Mariota played hurt that night, maybe 60 percent. Anyone who saw the Ducks quarterback refusing to run with open field in front of him, hobbling around the backfield, dragging his bad leg like a cane, knew it on sight.

When Marcus saw his father that night, he fell into his arms, and burst into tears. The two men hugged, and sobbed. And on Saturday, as Oregon pasted Stanford 45-16, it's that father-son scene I couldn't shake.

We've witnessed for months now, the kindness of Mariota. We've heard what a great teammate he is. We saw him stop to talk to children visiting from a hospital after the loss to Arizona earlier this season. We've heard from another hospital

patient who received a jersey from the quarterback, and we know he gives homeless people bottles of water and energy bars.

That stuff makes Mariota a great person. His athleticism makes him a great performer. But it's that tender scene with his father and the ensuing whipping he dealt to the Cardinal on Saturday that makes him a great competitor — maybe the greatest in college football.

"When Marcus gets to the point where he's yelling," Ducks receiver and special teams player, Austin Daich, said, "you'd better listen up."

Mariota had two good legs against Stanford on Saturday. He pummeled the Cardinal with them. He lashed Stanford with his arm, too. He ran for two touchdowns, and threw for two scores. His 258 passing yards weren't mind-blowing. His 19 of 30 passing night wasn't perfect. In fact, he threw an interception on what might have been his

---

ABOVE: Against Stanford, Marcus Mariota showed a side of himself openly displayed rarely — his intense competitiveness. Bruce Ely/The Oregonian/OregonLive

worst play of the season.

But it wasn't Mariota, the quarterback, who did the most damage. It was Mariota, the competitor. Even if he wouldn't say it.

"I guess I would have looked back after leaving here and regretted not beating them," he said.

He's soft selling it.

I saw Mariota with his father that night. In 20 years of doing this job, I've not witnessed a more authentic demonstration of pure emotion from an athlete. It was heart-wrenching, after the 26-20 loss that night, to watch Mariota wipe away the tears, his left knee in a brace (sprained MCL), and attempt to accept responsibility for an 8-0 record that melted into 8-1.

All that, "unfinished business," talk after he announced he was coming back for a junior season felt hinged to that long night.

On Saturday, Mariota punished Stanford. Not for beating him last season. But because this season they stood in his way. That's what a fierce competitor does. You can point to an offensive line that played physical, and running backs who ran with alacrity, but in the end, Mariota was the biggest difference between Oregon and Stanford. So much so, that if you swapped him and Kevin Hogan before kickoff, I'd give the Ducks no chance to win.

That uncharacteristic interception he threw? It was only the second this season for Mariota. It was just the 12th of his college career. And coach Mark Helfrich explained after that it came, he thought, because Mariota is so advanced, "he sometimes tries to run the receiver's route with

his throw."

He called him, "Mariota 5.05."

As if Mariota is a fifth-generation model of himself. Watching the replay, you could see the Stanford safety hanging over the top of the route and Mariota trying to make his receiver settle into the hole beyond the linebackers by underthrowing the pass.

Receiver kept running. Trailing defender didn't.

After the Mariota interception, Autzen Stadium hushed. What was this? A pick? A gift to the opponent from Mr. Nice Guy? It was as if everyone expected trumpets, and locusts, and horsemen to come next.

The Ducks not only improved their case to the College Football Playoff Selection Committee, but did so with the necessary style points. This is a beauty pageant now, and the Ducks were smiling, and posing, tiara in place. UO pinned 45 points on a Stanford program that hadn't given up as many since Oct. 2012 (vs. Arizona) in an overtime win.

Nice guy, this Mariota?

RIGHT: After losing two straight to Stanford, Mariota willed the Ducks to a win. Thomas Boyd/The Oregonian/OregonLive

You bet. After the game, Daich, a walk-on, redshirt sophomore, told a story about meeting Mariota for the first time a few years earlier. Their lockers were located directly across from each other. Daich had come from a small high school in Watsonville, California, an agricultural community with migrant workers and artichokes and lockers that are so small, Daich said, "I couldn't fit my helmet inside."

Mariota was the quarterback from Hawaii, a guy Oregon coveted. Daich's college choices came to this: A) a partial scholarship at San Jose State; or B) a chance to maybe play catch once in a while with Mariota. He chose Oregon. Mariota not only took the time to talk with Daich daily over the last few seasons, but Mariota even invited the walk-on to play golf alongside him.

"Even all the great stories you hear about him, you still don't feel like they can explain how good a person he is," Daich said. "The Heisman thing, most guys would let that go to their heads."

I wrote after the Arizona loss a month ago that Mariota's Heisman hopes were on the carpet at Autzen, in pieces. Wrong. The quarterback calmly collected the fragments and fashioned them into a sharpened spear that he just drove into Stanford's chest. He's not only back, but the Heisman Trust should just give him the trophy now.

The manner with which he's roared back says so much about him. The way he's followed that loss with consistency and grit, punctuates who he is. Maybe it was coincidental, but I received my initial contact envelope from the Heisman body 24 hours in front of the latest Mariota performance.

I don't need to see another snap. This is the guy. He has my vote. The only thing anybody should be unsure of at this point is who to put No. 2 and 3 on the ballot.

Last season, that Stanford loss, and that limited Mariota, was all the rest of the voting nation had to go on. This season, everyone who bothers to watch is seeing what Mariota is capable of on a regular basis.

After Saturday's victory over Stanford, I saw Mariota's family waiting for him outside the locker room. He was inside, dressed in cargo shorts and a T-shirt, finishing his postgame interviews. He credited his offensive line, and his teammates, and said complimentary things about Stanford.

It's not his legs, or his arm, that beats teams. It's not even his brain.

It's his will.

Mess with that, and you get the horns. ∎

LEFT: Lauded for his own talents, Mariota is quick to pass the adulation on to his teammates.

Bruce Ely/The Oregonian/OregonLive

#4 OREGON 51, #17 UTAH 27

DUCKS BOOSTED BY CLAY-BRAINED PLAY

Oregon escapes Utah with 51-27 victory, its title hopes still within reach thanks to improbable play

ANDREW GREIF
THE OREGONIAN/OREGONLIVE

SALT LAKE CITY — Utah had an upset of Oregon, and impending chaos in the College Football Playoff race, seemingly right in its hands.

And then Kaelin Clay dropped it.

In a 51-27 slugfest at Rice-Eccles Stadium on Saturday night, where yards did not come easily, leads were tenuous and injuries mounted for fifth-ranked Oregon at crucial positions, a fumble on the easiest play Utah had all night changed the course of the game — and possibly the Ducks' season.

"Definitely not a garden-variety 51-27 win," head coach Mark Helfrich said.

RIGHT: A wide-open Kaelin Clay snags a pass from teammate Travis Wilson and heads for the end zone. Clay's apparent 78-yard touchdown was negated, however, when he put the ball on the turf a yard short of the goal line. Thomas Boyd/The Oregonian/OregonLive

OPPOSITE: A convoy of blockers escorts Oregon's Joe Walker after he picked up the live ball Clay had left on the field. Walker's 100-yard return gave Oregon a 7-7 tie instead of what appeared to be a two-touchdown deficit.

Thomas Boyd/The Oregonian/OregonLive

They clinched the Pac-12 North division and kept national championship hopes alive thanks to a gutsy five-play, 75-yard drive with 10:29 remaining that included bulldozing runs by Royce Freeman, a left knee injury to All-American center Hroniss Grasu and a 34-yard touchdown pass to Dwayne Stanford to take a 37-27 lead.

"Poise," safety Erick Dargan said of the attitude when Utah cut the lead to three. "Don't panic."

The Ducks added two more touchdowns later in the fourth quarter to turn a tight game into a blowout.

After the bizarre events two quarters prior that Oregon drive, such a dramatic parry wouldn't have seemed necessary.

Not after Utah suffered a demoralizing twist of fortune when Clay, the Utes' speedy

receiver and kick returner, got behind Oregon's secondary for a 78-yard reception and certain touchdown — until he fumbled at the 2-yard line while prematurely celebrating the score and an imminent 14-0 Utah lead.

While Clay played to the crowd in the back of the end zone, Dargan noticed the ball was live a few beats later, and after Dargan was tangled near the goal line, the ball popped into middle linebacker Joe Walker's hands. He returned the inexplicable error 100 yards for a touchdown, becoming just the fifth player in college football history to do so and second this season, after Washington's Shaq Thompson.

"Usually when you score a touchdown they put their hands up and signal and I didn't see it," Dargan said. "Me and the ref made eye contact. It was an awkward moment like, I'm just going to pick the ball up and try to go with it."

Just your average 14-point, 178-yard swing.

Yet in the face of the fumble and injuries that knocked starting quarterback Kendal Thompson and receiver Tim Patrick out of the game, the Utes twice cut into 14-point Duck leads. Only when Ducks corner Troy Hill ran back an interception of Travis Wilson to the Utah 11 with 4:31 remaining was a win ensured.

The win came at a cost.

Grasu walked off the field under his own power, slowly, after appearing to injure a left knee. He didn't return and was replaced by Doug Brenner. All-American cornerback Ifo Ekpre-Olomu wore a protective boot on his left foot after hurting his big toe, he said.

"I'm not really too concerned," Ekpre-Olomu said, adding he expects to play against Colorado on Nov. 22.

TOP RIGHT: It was another big night for Marcus Mariota. Besides passing for 239 yards and three touchdowns, Mariota also led the team in rushing with 114 yards and one score. Thomas Boyd/The Oregonian/OregonLive

BOTTOM RIGHT: All Dwayne Stanford (88) did at Utah was catch touchdown passes. Stanford had two receptions for the night, but both were for scores — 3 yards in the second quarter and 34 yards in the fourth.
Thomas Boyd/The Oregonian/OregonLive

OPPOSITE: In what proved to be his last game of the season, tight end Pharaoh Brown caught three passes for 40 yards and this touchdown before he was seriously injured in the fourth quarter and carried from the field.
Thomas Boyd/The Oregonian/OregonLive

And in a fitting but hard-to-watch picture of Oregon's night, when it suffered even in victory, star tight end Pharaoh Brown was carted off in the fourth quarter, injured blocking for quarterback Marcus Mariota's 1-yard touchdown run to take a 44-27 lead. He later left the stadium in an ambulance, on a stretcher.

Mariota finished with 114 rushing yards and one touchdown, 239 passing yards and three touchdowns, completing 17-of-29 attempts without an interception, and lost a fumble. On a night when his offensive line allowed four sacks — as many as it had given up in its previous four games combined — Mariota's movement outside of a rapidly shrinking pocket kept the offense in motion, too, for 508 total yards. He masked Oregon's 4-of-13 performance on third down.

Freshmen shined for Oregon, with Freeman rushing for 99 yards and a touchdown, and walk-on kicker Aidan Schneider nailing all three of his field goal attempts, including from a career-long 42.

Utah (6-3, 3-3 Pac-12) running back Devontae Booker was held to 65 rushing yards, less than half his season average, but hurt Oregon's secondary with 110 receiving yards, including a 28-yard touchdown to pull Utah within 27-20. The Utes got within 30-27 on a 13-yard touchdown pass by Wilson, who was intercepted twice after entering with an unblemished interception line.

The Ducks (9-1, 6-1) were not alone in their struggle. Top-10 teams dragged themselves off the turf Saturday, with Auburn losing, Alabama escaping in overtime at LSU and Kansas State

---

OPPOSITE: Oregon's defense held Utah back Devontae Booker to 65 yards rushing, half his season average, but Booker also had eight pass receptions for 110 yards and a touchdown. Thomas Boyd/The Oregonian/OregonLive

TOP LEFT: Royce Freeman's 99 yards helped an Oregon rushing game that ground out 269 yards, 154 of them coming in the second half. Thomas Boyd/The Oregonian/OregonLive

BOTTOM LEFT: Oregon's DeForest Bucker (44) and Arik Armstead celebrate one of walk-on kicker Aidan Schneider's three field goals, including a career-long 42-yarder. Thomas Boyd/The Oregonian/OregonLive

getting routed by TCU. UO has a bye before closing with Colorado and Oregon State.

No matter the improbable bounces that it took to do so, Oregon's ultimate goal remains within reach.

"You never want a game to turn on something like that," offensive coordinator Scott Frost said of Clay's fumble-turned-TD. "I'm glad we got the win, I'm glad it worked out the way it did, I feel sorry for them. That's a mistake that you can't make and happy that our guys recognized it and capitalized." ■

OPPOSITE: Senior center Hroniss Grasu, who had started every game of his Oregon career, walks off the field with an apparent knee injury, accompanied by trainers and quarterback Mariota. Thomas Boyd/The Oregonian/OregonLive

TOP LEFT: Mariota led the Ducks in both passing and rushing and scored on a one-yard run in the fourth quarter — the same play on which tight end Brown was injured. Thomas Boyd/The Oregonian/OregonLive

BOTTOM LEFT: Stanford stretches for the goal line at the end of his 34-yard pass reception that pushed Oregon's lead to 37-27 in the third quarter after Utah had rallied to within three points. Thomas Boyd/The Oregonian/OregonLive

AUTZEN SAYS 'MAHALO'

Oregon overwhelms Colorado, sending seniors — and maybe Marcus Mariota — out in style, 44-10

ANDREW GREIF
THE OREGONIAN/OREGONLIVE

EUGENE — If this was goodbye, it was magnificent — and soaked in significance.

In what could be Oregon quarterback Marcus Mariota's final game at Autzen Stadium before a jump to the NFL, the junior Heisman Trophy candidate's four touchdowns ripped through the record book and Colorado's overmatched defense in a 44-10 victory on a wet Saturday that began with Oregon staffers handing out green-and-yellow leis and saying "mahalo" to many of the 55,891 on hand, a nod to Mariota's Hawaiian roots.

It ended with Oregon's seventh consecutive 10-win season, a standing-ovation for the

QB, whose 42 total touchdowns this season surpassed USC's Matt Barkley for a new Pac-12 Conference record, and with a reminder that this is far from the end for Mariota's time with the Ducks.

If they play like they did Saturday, they could find themselves in four more games.

"We have a lot of games left and we can't get caught in this moment," said Mariota, who was 24-of-32 passing for 324 yards and gained 73 rushing yards on eight carries. "We just kept focusing on what's ahead, you can never let the moment get too big for you."

Without saying whether he will return for his

OPPOSITE: Marcus Mariota leaves the field at Autzen stadium, likely for the last time.
Bruce Ely/The Oregonian/OregonLive

RIGHT: Mark Helfrich was Oregon's offensive coordinator and quarterbacks coach when he saw film of Mariota as a junior at Saint Louis High School in Honolulu. Helfrich went to Hawaii to see Mariota in person and the Ducks offered him a scholarship on the spot. It was Mariota's only scholarship offer. Bruce Ely/The Oregonian/OregonLive

senior season, Mariota acknowledged he was taking "mental pictures" on the sideline on the advice of his family and coaches. But it was he who left those watching with some indelible images, too.

After freshman Royce Freeman opened the game with one of his two rushing touchdowns, Mariota dashed 46 yards around the right side on a read-option, untouched. That put him in a class with Nevada's Colin Kaepernick and Cody Fajardo, Florida's Tim Tebow, Baylor's Robert Griffin III and Central Michigan's Dan LeFevour as the sixth Football Bowl Subdivision player with 9,000 career passing yards and 2,000 rushing yards.

He followed with a 31-yard touchdown pass to Charles Nelson in the second quarter, a 15-yard touchdown to tight end Evan Baylis in the third and closed with a 14-yard dart to Nelson that provided the final margin.

His final snap was a 1-yard handoff with 13:21 remaining in the fourth quarter to Kenny Bassett before Jeff Lockie, his backup and roommate, replaced him to cheers.

"I still get to spend a lot of time around him

OPPOSITE: The Ducks take the field against Colorado. Bruce Ely/The Oregonian/OregonLive

TOP LEFT: There was too much Mariota for Colorado. Mariota completed 24 of 32 passes for 323 yards and three touchdowns. Bruce Ely/The Oregonian/OregonLive

BOTTOM LEFT: Royce Freeman gets 20 of his 105 yards rushing on this first-quarter touchdown jaunt. Freeman became the first Ducks freshman to rush for more than 1,000 yards in a season. Bruce Ely/The Oregonian/OregonLive

before this whole thing is done," said offensive coordinator Scott Frost, whose unit had 597 yards, punted just three times and was 9-of-15 on third down. "I told him before the game I'm not going to get emotional for him until we're all through but he has a special place in my heart and my life."

Freeman, meanwhile, became the first UO true freshman with 1,000 yards by rushing for 105. And he is now fifth all-time for No. 3 Oregon (10-1, 7-1 Pac-12, College Football Playoff No. 2), with 16 rushing touchdowns.

As sweet as it was for Mariota, it was a forgettable day to be a quarterback for Colorado (2-9, 0-8).

Sophomore Jordan Gehrke earned his first career start in place of Sefo Liufau and struggled to find rhythm. To wit: At the end of the first quarter, Mariota's 61 rushing yards were six more than Colorado's total yards. Liufau took over in the second half, not that it changed anything. CU's 226 yards and 10 points were its fewest this season.

"Probably our most solid effort all year, start to finish," head coach Mark Helfrich said.

The defense was most evident on the perimeter, where star wideout Nelson Spruce caught two passes for 16 yards after entering with an FBS-leading 9.9 catches per game. Corner Troy Hill glued himself to Spruce and had help when Oregon rolled other defenders his way, trying to confuse the young QBs. But it started up front, where the front seven blunted the running game and forced CU to pass.

"The interior was really solid," defensive coordinator Don Pellum said. "I don't think the other team tried to continue to run it in there because it wasn't happening."

The sight of defensive tackle DeForest Buckner writhing on the turf was one of few scares, though the junior defensive lineman walked off under his own power.

Mariota's own walk off the field, to cheers and chants of "MAR-I-O-TA" from the student section, will be remembered most from Saturday, however.

One of the first to meet him was Grasu, who'd snapped to Mariota in every game of his career until Saturday. On the sideline, they looked backward, and forward. Next week is Oregon State in the 118th Civil War.

OPPOSITE: Late in the first quarter, Mariota took off untouched and went 46 yards for a touchdown, capping a 54-yard scoring drive that took all of 47 seconds to complete. Bruce Ely/The Oregonian/OregonLive

LEFT: Marcus Mariota celebrates what may be his final rushing touchdown in Autzen stadium. Bruce Ely/The Oregonian/OregonLive

"I just told him thank you for all the memories I've had of him, all the memories of this entire team, this senior class, he's special to us," Grasu said. "And I told him now you better get ready for the Beavers." ■

TOP RIGHT: Oregon's pass defense, led here by Reggie Daniels and Ifo Ekpre-Olomu (14) had Colorado receivers covered up all day. Bruce Ely/The Oregonian/OregonLive

BOTTOM RIGHT: Speedy freshman Charles Nelson stepped up with three pass receptions for 62 yards and two touchdowns. Bruce Ely/The Oregonian/OregonLive

OPPOSITE: Darren Carrington showed what has become his trademark — a spectacular, acrobatic catch in coverage. Bruce Ely/The Oregonian/OregonLive

BELOW: If Mariota has played his last game at Autzen Stadium, his last snap was a handoff to Kenny Bassett that gained a yard. Bruce Ely/The Oregonian/OregonLive

CHAIN SAW WAS IN THE DUCKS' HANDS

*Oregon Ducks shred Oregon State a
7th straight year in 47-19 Civil War rout*

ANDREW GREIF
THE OREGONIAN/OREGONLIVE

CORVALLIS — In a clear and cold Reser Stadium, the chainsaw's roar was heard most often on third down Saturday evening, a signal piped in at ear-splitting volume for the fans to get loud, and the defense to get stout.

Except junior quarterback Marcus Mariota's Heisman Trophy candidacy and Oregon's national championship dreams were the furthest thing from shredded Saturday evening.

Instead, it was the Ducks who put the Beavers through a wood chipper.

Oregon's 47-19 victory earned a seventh consecutive win this season and a seventh straight win in the Civil War series with an ease that sucked the sound out of the stadium except for the saw's plaintive rev.

The game was over at halftime and the majority of the 45,722 who left and didn't return for the second half knew it. With it went Oregon State's season, falling one win short of bowl eligibility at 5-7.

The Ducks scored on their first five drives with an efficiency that served as a signal that, no, this team wasn't looking ahead to next week's Pac-12 championship game rematch with Arizona.

When Oregon emerged from its team meetings Friday afternoon to learn Arizona had won the

---

OPPOSITE: Showing his superior athleticism in what may be his final Civil War game, Marcus Mariota hurdles OSU's Justin Strong. Bruce Ely/The Oregonian/OregonLive

RIGHT: Mariota overshadowed Sean Mannion, his Oregon State counterpart, passing for 367 yards and four TDs and rushing for two more scores.
Randy L. Rasmussen/The Oregonian/OregonLive

South Division, "People were just like, 'Oh, I guess we're playing Arizona in the Pac-12,'" center Hamani Stevens said with a half-hearted shrug, revealing little revenge stemming from Oregon's lone loss this season. "That was about it."

Mariota completed 19 of 25 passes for 367 yards and four touchdowns and ran for two more scores, making the Beavers' senior-laden defense resemble a speed bump as it became a footnote to history: Mariota eclipsed 4,000 yards of total offense and Oregon reached 11 wins for the sixth

time in school history and the fifth consecutive season.

"He missed a couple throws today, unbelievable," head coach Mark Helfrich said, in mock disdain. "That guy is such a stud."

Offensive coordinator Scott Frost, whose unit piled up 565 yards, used another word to describe freshman running back Royce Freeman after his fifth 100-yard rushing game this season went for 135 yards (he added a 12-yard receiving touchdown, too).

"He's an unusual freshman, and he's going to have an unbelievable career," Frost said. "We're lucky to have him."

Oregon ripped off 8.7 yards per play, which was actually a dropoff from the double-digits UO averaged well into the third quarter, thanks to scoring plays such as a 77-yard pass from Mariota to Byron Marshall, 29- and 27-yard passes from Mariota to Charles Nelson and a 23-yard Mariota dash.

"It really helps when you can start out fast in Corvallis," Mariota said. "The crowd just kind of quieted down a little bit."

When the chainsaw tried to create noise on third down, Oregon converted the hard yards with preposterous ease, averaging more than 24.5 yards on third down in the first half as it piled up a 30-3 halftime lead. In the third quarter, Mariota walked in from one yard out on fourth down to extend the mismatch to 40-10.

The Beavers found trouble even getting one yard, twice going for it on fourth down in the first half before being stopped short by a push from Oregon's defensive line and finished by hits from safety Reggie Daniels and linebacker Rodney Hardrick.

"I think we played smart, and from a defensive standpoint we gave up more running yardage in situations than we wanted to, but I think a lot of the other things they wanted to do on offense we were able to counter," defensive coordinator Don Pellum said. "... We gave up some plays, but we were able to get stops."

Oregon State running back Storm Woods, held out of practice much the week with an undisclosed injury, ran for 128 yards and a touchdown, but the vaunted deep-passing game never found its timing, with Jordan Villamin and Victor Bolden combining for 28 yards.

This was a rout.

Next comes a rematch, with a Pac-12 title on the line.

"(Arizona) beat us twice, but Stanford beat us twice and we put a good whooping on them," said Marshall, who had 131 receiving yards and six catches. "Hopefully the same thing happens." ■

OPPOSITE: Royce Freeman rushed for 135 yards on 22 carries, but got this touchdown as a receiver on a 12-yard pass from Mariota. Bruce Ely/The Oregonian/OregonLive

LEFT: Charles Nelson had only 17 pass receptions in 2014, but five of them were for touchdowns. He had two catches against OSU, but they produced the game's first touchdown and its last. Bruce Ely/The Oregonian/OregonLive

RIGHT: As Oregon State defenders get tangled up, Byron Marshall reels in a pass from Mariota that turned into a 77-yard touchdown that gave Oregon a 23-0 lead early in the second quarter. Bruce Ely/The Oregonian/OregonLive

BOTTOM LEFT: As he did so many times during the season, Mariota finished the Civil War on the bench with the game won and the reserves on the field.
Bruce Ely/The Oregonian/OregonLive

BOTTOM RIGHT: Mariota's 23-yard touchdown run in the second quarter made it 30-0 Oregon and made the final score the game's only remaining uncertainty.
Bruce Ely/The Oregonian/OregonLive

LEFT: Oregon State's pass rush managed four sacks of Mariota, totaling 19 yards in losses.

Bruce Ely/The Oregonian/OregonLive

BOTTOM LEFT: Fans adopted a variation of a quote from a Catholic schoolboy in Eugene discussing the three most important topics among his friends.

Bruce Ely/The Oregonian/OregonLive

BOTTOM RIGHT: With the game over, Mariota took time to greet friends and family members in attendance — including his mom, Alana Deppe-Mariota.

Bruce Ely/The Oregonian/OregonLive

#2 OREGON 51, #7 ARIZONA 13

DUCKS TRAVEL THE EASY ROUT

Oregon Ducks earn Pac-12 championship and likely clinch berths in College Football Playoff, Heisman Trophy winner's circle

ANDREW GREIF
THE OREGONIAN/OREGONLIVE

SANTA CLARA, Calif. — The Ducks earned their revenge, all right.

And a Pac-12 championship.

And — barring an unforeseen event — a berth in the first four-team College Football Playoff along with the Heisman Trophy for quarterback Marcus Mariota.

Nine weeks after a home defeat to Arizona put Oregon's vast potential in doubt, Mark Helfrich's Ducks roared back with an equally staggering display of defense and dominance Friday night in Levi's Stadium, earning their first conference title since 2011 by routing Arizona, 51-13.

Officially, Mariota doused Helfrich with a cel-

ebratory bucket of green-tinted Gatorade at the 31-yard line with 13 seconds remaining. But after Oregon's defense held Arizona to just 25 yards on 25 first-half plays and its offense provided a 23-0 halftime lead, the celebration could have begun two quarters earlier.

What was billed as essentially a playoff

quarterfinal between the playoff's No. 2 and No. 7-ranked teams resembled an early-season blowout.

"Arizona got the better of us this season," Helfrich said of Oregon's Oct. 2 loss. "We never looked back from it."

Mariota overcame an uncharacteristically

OPPOSITE: With the conference championship in their pocket, the Ducks' postgame meeting at Levi's Stadium was all about trophies and confetti.
Thomas Boyd/The Oregonian/OregonLive

RIGHT: As the clock wound down on Oregon's Pac-12 championship, Marcus Mariota and lineman Hamani Stevens gave coach Mark Helfrich the traditional Gatorade shower. Thomas Boyd/The Oregonian/OregonLive

slow start to turn in another typically commanding game, rushing for three touchdowns and passing for two more while clinching his first conference title — one of the few accomplishments missing from his historic resume. He now has 101 career passing touchdowns, moving past USC's Matt Leinart for second-most in Pac-12 history. In all, he accounted for 336 yards.

"If this guy isn't what the Heisman Trophy is all about," Helfrich said, "I'm in the wrong profession."

"Thanks, coach," Mariota deadpanned.

Though word of Oregon's entrance in the playoff won't come until Sunday morning, and Mariota's trip to the Heisman ceremony in New York City won't be confirmed until a day later, each was all but clinched during Oregon's eighth consecutive victory and 12th win overall, matching a program record.

Mariota held a rose as he was named title game MVP, a symbol of where his team is likely headed on New Year's Day for a playoff semifinal. It would be a symbolic venue for the Ducks, too, as their leave-no-doubt winning streak — its average margin of victory during that span is 26 points — began in Pasadena.

"It's a different team this time of year,"

Helfrich said. "We have elevated in a bunch of different ways. There are a bunch of big smiles and I'm proud of that."

Though statistics will show Oregon (12-1) rolled up 640 yards on an Arizona (10-3) defense that had stymied it during the teams' past two meetings, both Wildcat wins, this victory truly started with the defense.

UO cornerback Ifo Ekpre-Olomu forced a fumble on Arizona's first kickoff return and safety Tyree Robinson recovered, which led to Oregon's second field goal in as many drives.

Arizona gave the ball back to Oregon either via punt or turnover on downs on its next eight drives, and had 224 yards on 61 plays, by far the Ducks defense's best game under first-year coordinator Don Pellum. The play of the defense bought valuable time for Oregon's offense as it found its own rhythm. It moved the ball at will until it entered the red zone; its first four trips inside the Arizona 20-yard line yielded six points, a missed field goal and a turnover on downs.

Then, like body blows, Oregon yards, points and stops piled up in a brutally efficient combination.

Consider that Mariota didn't throw an incomplete pass after halftime, going 11 of 11. One of those passes was a 46-yard laser to Darren Carrington thrown off one foot while running

---

LEFT: Royce Freeman rushed for 114 yards and often had Arizona off balance and out of position.

Thomas Boyd/The Oregonian/OregonLive

BELOW: The ball bounced right for Byron Marshall, who had Oregon's sole fumble of the evening, which the Ducks recovered. Thomas Boyd/The Oregonian/OregonLive

to his right after escaping an ankle tackle by conference defensive player of the year Scooby Wright, the Arizona linebacker.

Defensive lineman DeForest Buckner repeatedly bulled through an Arizona offensive line with 166 combined starts, leading Oregon with seven tackles. Safety Erick Dargan intercepted his team-leading sixth pass and the Ducks' defense didn't allow a snap inside its own red zone.

Meanwhile, Arizona coach Rich Rodriguez's opening statement to his postgame press conference said it all about the Wildcats' frustration:

"Wasn't a good night."

Freshman running back Royce Freeman gained 137 yards, while receivers Carrington and Charles Nelson accounted for 126 and 104 receiving yards, respectively, thanks to big plays.

Nelson's 73-yard reception in the second quarter set up Oregon's second touchdown, a four-yard run by Mariota into the end zone's left corner, directly in front of Oregon's cheering section (one of few full sections in a stadium with large swaths of empty, red seats).

"We had a lot of motivation coming into this game," Mariota said. "We just wanted to go out and play the best game that we could."

That game earned them the school's fourth conference championship since 2009 Friday night.

And it put them on track for potentially much, much more. ■

TOP LEFT: Oregon's Torrodney Prevot gets a sack of Arizona quarterback Anu Solomon. A native of Hawaii, like Mariota, and a big part of the Wildcats earlier win over the Ducks, Solomon and the Arizona offense could do little against Oregon this time around.

Thomas Boyd/The Oregonian/OregonLive

TOP RIGHT: Wide receiver Keanon Lowe loses his helmet but not possession on his only touch of the ball for the game, a nine-yard run to the Arizona 4-yard-line that set up a Mariota rushing touchdown on the next play.

Thomas Boyd/The Oregonian/OregonLive

RIGHT: Wide receiver Charles Nelson became a force for the Ducks, with seven pass receptions for 104 yards.

Thomas Boyd/The Oregonian/OregonLive

LEFT: Oregon sacked Arizona's Solomon three times during the game with Prevot, DeForest Buckner and Tony Washington getting one each.

Thomas Boyd/The Oregonian/OregonLive

BOTTOM LEFT: Mariota's 38 pass attempts in the game were a season high, but he completed 25 of them for 313 yards and two touchdowns. When he came out of the game in the fourth quarter, Oregon led 44-7.

Thomas Boyd/The Oregonian/OregonLive

BOTTOM RIGHT: Saving his best for the title game, freshman Nelson had season bests in both pass receptions and yards gained. He also returned two kickoffs for a 25.5 yard average.

Thomas Boyd/The Oregonian/OregonLive

OPPOSITE: Marcus Mariota celebrates a second quarter touchdown, one of three rushing touchdowns for the day. Thomas Boyd/The Oregonian/OregonLive

LEFT: With Arizona safety Jared Tevis in no position to stop him, Mariota takes off into the open field. Thomas Boyd/The Oregonian/OregonLive

BOTTOM LEFT: Receiver Darren Carrington finished the regular season with 30 catches for 539 yards and two touchdowns, including this one on an 11-yard pass from Mariota that made it 37-7. Thomas Boyd/The Oregonian/OregonLive

BELOW: Byron Marshall was Oregon's leading receiver with 61 receptions for 814 yards. He also had 383 rushing yards, fourth-best on the team, and scored six touchdowns combined. Thomas Boyd/The Oregonian/OregonLive

ABOVE: Back in the end zone again, Mariota hands the football to an official after scoring one of his three rushing touchdowns against Arizona. Thomas Boyd/The Oregonian/OregonLive

RIGHT: Mariota gets a boost from lineman Matt Pierson and support from Jake Pisarcik (76) after rushing for a score. Mariota scored 14 rushing touchdowns this season, second nationally among FBS quarterbacks. Thomas Boyd/The Oregonian/OregonLive

OPPOSITE: Prevot (86), Troy Hill (13) and teammates whoop it up on the field at Levi's Stadium after time expires and the Ducks secure their fourth conference championship in six seasons. Thomas Boyd/The Oregonian/OregonLive

LEFT: Oregon fans made up the majority of the announced crowd of 45,618 at Levi's Stadium in Santa Clara, Calif. It was the second-smallest crowd to witness an Oregon game during the 2014 season. Thomas Boyd/The Oregonian/OregonLive

BELOW: Oregon players gather around the Pac-12 trophy in their dressing room at Levi's Stadium. The win vaulted the Ducks into the College Football Playoff and a date with Florida State at the Rose Bowl in Pasadena on New Year's Day. Thomas Boyd/The Oregonian/OregonLive

Ducks' talent bonds, forming a team that looks like No. 1

John Canzano
The Oregonian/OregonLive

SANTA CLARA, Calif. — He'd won nothing yet. No conference championship. No Heisman Trophy. No Johnny Unitas Award. No nothing.

Maybe Marcus Mariota sped around Levi's Stadium in the second half like a guy whose feet barely touched turf because he was playing with a couple of empty pockets on Friday night.

Oregon blistered Arizona 51-13 to win the Pac-12 championship. Mariota threw for 313 yards, and accounted for five touchdowns (three rushing, two passing). And while this wasn't as graceful as a ballet or as fluid as the symphony — the Ducks had 13 penalties and started the game by littering field goals all over the place — the victory ends up a booming statement by a program that badly needed to make one.

The College Football Playoff selection committee gathered in Dallas and watched the conference title game as a group. They'll also watch Alabama play Missouri on Saturday in the SEC Championship. But as a prelude the committee

watched one-loss UO untie the ugly knot Arizona put in the Ducks' schedule at Autzen Stadium in Week 5.

Now, had the Ducks simply executed this task as if they were taking out the trash, it would have been fine. The UA demon would have been exorcized. The questions about that seven-point loss would have been answered. The past would have been the past.

In fact, the Ducks started the game so tight, so sputtering, so inexplicably sloppy to start, that anyone who watched them began to wonder if they knew America was watching.

Then, Mariota and his teammates got busy mak-

ing a statement.

No. 2 Oregon rolled out a convincing case for itself as the No. 1 team in America. Current top-ranked Alabama will have an opportunity to answer on Saturday. But with 640 yards of offense, and 31 first downs, and 51 blistering points on a neutral field, this was a back-alley whipping pulled center stage.

Arizona, the No. 7 team in the playoff rankings, was shut out until the third quarter, and didn't score its final six points until the last play of regulation. It looked anemic, lifeless and done. Linebacker Scooby Wright tossed his snacks on the sideline. Quarterback Anu Solomon looked skittish. Coach Rich Rodriguez had no answers, especially when he was asked for a statement after the game.

"That wasn't a good night," he said. "Next (question)."

If this game were an election, it would have been called late in the second quarter. The state of Arizona hasn't seen this sort of thrashing since LBJ went four-wide and rolled Barry Goldwater (R-AZ) in the 1964 presidential election 44-6 in states won.

"Sometimes you refer to the skill guys, but it's not just the skill guys," Rodriguez said. "They're very athletic across the board."

Now. To be fair. Anyone who has watched Mariota-led Oregon this season knows the quarterback and his teammates had an "off" night to start. He threw 13 incompletions, every one of them in the first half. He missed some throws he normally makes. He appeared to be pressing for the first time since anyone can remember. He just looked — off. But then, the second half started

and Mariota pulled out the surgeon's scalpel.

After the break, Mariota was a perfect 11 of 11 for 123 yards and two touchdown passes. He darted, and dashed, and looked again like the best college football player in America. Mariota was asked in the preseason by Oregon's athletic department staff if he wanted them to mount a Heisman Trophy campaign for him this season. After all, he'd given UO the gift of coming back for a junior season, and the possibilities were low-hanging fruit.

"No thanks," came Mariota's answer.

He'd mount that campaign himself, thank you.

The playoff selection committee has an unenviable task. We all know they have a difficult decision with the No. 4 team. But what Oregon did on Friday was give the 13-member committee a headache at the top, especially even should Alabama win but fail to look dominating against Missouri.

That top seed matters because Florida State feels like the No. 4 team, and the easiest out in the semifinal round. The Seminoles are the defending champions, and have the reigning Heisman winner at quarterback. They're winners, and undefeated, but they're also ripe.

What's changed at Oregon since week No. 5?

Nobody wants to play them anymore.

The Ducks are healthier at some key positions, and vastly improved at some others. They're humming now, as always on offense, but especially now on defense. They've come through that home defeat that raised so many questions not by unraveling but by galvanizing — like fingers forming a fist. And Mariota is the big knuckle, right in the middle.

Oregon knows how to win.

It's that simple.

"It's a different team this time of year," Ducks coach Mark Helfrich said.

Helfrich deserves a boatload of credit for pulling this group together. It was not just talent, but coaching, and leadership, that results in a ride like this. Only question now is whether he can finish the parade with a bow in Jerryworld.

These Ducks know what winning big tastes like now. They know what it smells like. They know how to do the little things that result in victory. It's the same feel and formula that Florida State patented last season on the way to that title game victory over Auburn.

In fact, after the game, during the trophy presentation, the sight from high above is the one that fans needed to see. As I wrote this paragraph, looking down from the eighth level of Levi's Stadium, watching UO accept its trophy, the most interesting sight developed. As the Ducks stood on that platform in the end zone together, there was plenty of space behind them and around the edges. But they stood so tightly packed you couldn't see any space between them.

This was a team.

One that just made a case for the No. 1 ranking. ■

OPPOSITE: Marcus Mariota let his performances do the talking in the campaign for the Heisman and all other awards. Thomas Boyd/The Oregonian/OregonLive

LEFT: Mariota would finish the regular season on the bench, watching Jeff Lockie complete the win over Arizona. Thomas Boyd/The Oregonian/OregonLive

HEISMAN VOTE A SNAP FOR DUCK

Marcus Mariota makes history, winning Oregon Ducks' first Heisman Trophy

BY ANDREW GREIF
THE OREGONIAN/OREGONLIVE

NEW YORK — Marcus Mariota, the transcendent Oregon Ducks junior quarterback recruited out of near anonymity from Hawaii, pushed his program to its high-water mark Saturday night under the brightest of lights in Times Square by earning its first Heisman Trophy in a landslide.

"I am honored to be standing here," Mariota said after gathering himself at the podium. "This award belongs to my teammates. The amount of sacrifice they have made is not unnoticed."

Famously uncomfortable discussing his own accomplishments, Mariota's acceptance speech was dotted instead with thanks to his parents, Toa and Alana, his brother, Matt, Oregon's defense, his offensive teammates, the city of Eugene, his coaches, past teachers, Nike co-founder Phil Knight and his wife, Penny, and his

---

OPPOSITE: Wearing leis bestowed upon him by friends and family, Oregon quarterback Marcus Mariota speaks at a press conference after winning the Heisman Trophy.
Thomas Boyd/The Oregonian/OregonLive

RIGHT: Mariota meets with fans as he leaves the Best Buy Theater in New York City following the Heisman presentation ceremony. Thomas Boyd/The Oregonian/OregonLive

fellow alumni of Honolulu's St. Louis High in a moment that left him and those in the Best Buy Theatre emotional.

Though unflappable all week during his awards circuit, and just as comfortable facing blitzes and coverages, Mariota fought back tears as he made his remarks.

"It was moving," UO athletic director Rob Mullens said of the speech. "The whole room was crying. I'm sitting facing the stage, I've got tears in my eyes, I'm looking at a camera man who's not even watching and he's wiping tears from his eyes."

The award, considered the highest individual

honor in college football, is the first to go to a non-USC player from the West Coast since 1970, when the famed stiff-arm trophy went to Stanford's Jim Plunkett — the very man who sat next to Mariota during the ceremony.

It caps an unprecedented week for Mariota, who still has not lost a national award he was nominated for this season. On Monday, he earned the Johnny Unitas Golden Arm Award. On Thursday, he won the Davey O'Brien Quarterback award and Walter Camp and Maxwell awards for player of the year.

Mariota earned more than double the points of fellow finalists Melvin Gordon, the Wisconsin running back, and Amari Cooper, the Alabama receiver, in a night that was less about suspense than learning the final margin in Mariota's favor.

On the ballots of 929 voters, Mariota had 2,534 points and won by 1,284 points over Gordon while earning 90.9 percent of possible points — only Ohio State's Troy Smith in 2006 had a more convincing victory.

Mariota won all six regions of voters by wide margins and totaled 788 first-place votes.

This season he passed for 3,773 yards, 38 touchdowns and two interceptions while completing 68.3 percent of his passes. He also rushed for 669 yards and 14 touchdowns and caught a touchdown pass. His 53 total touchdowns set a Pac-12 single-season record.

"In Hawaii, if one person is successful the entire state is successful," said Mariota, who entered his press conference wearing several leis, a nod to his home state that now can boast a Heisman winner. "To be part of that is so special.

"We have talent. ... I hope this is just the begin-ning. I hope kids back home find the courage to continue to do this and maybe we'll have another (Heisman)."

Mariota's victory achieves what only a handful of Ducks had ever come close to reaching, but what no one had won.

Quarterback Norm Van Brocklin finished sixth

BELOW LEFT: Mariota wears a No. 19 Johnny Unitas Baltimore Colts jersey as he tours the Sports Legends at Camden Yards Museum in Baltimore on Dec. 12 as part of winning the 2014 Johnny Unitas Golden Arm Award.

Thomas Boyd/The Oregonian/OregonLive

BELOW RIGHT: After the Heisman Trophy presentation Dec. 13, Mariota meets the media in New York City.

Thomas Boyd/The Oregonian/OregonLive

in 1948. Quarterback George Shaw was seventh in 1954. In 2007 Dennis Dixon was, like Mariota, a dynamic spread-offense quarterback and Heisman favorite in November whose campaign crumpled under the weight of torn knee ligaments. He finished fifth.

Even Mariota himself had endured Heisman hurt before, when he fell from frontrunner in November 2013 to out of the top 10 in the voting last season as he hurt his knee and Oregon lost two games down the stretch.

"I think he deserved to be in New York last year," offensive coordinator Scott Frost said. "People are fickle anymore and it's what have you done for me lately, but I've got a ton of respect for the two other kids who are here and what they've accomplished. But I don't think there was any doubt who the best player in the country was."

Before Mariota, only two Ducks had made the trip to New York as finalists. Quarterback Joey Harrington was fourth in 2001 behind the thrust of a national publicity campaign. Running back LaMichael James ran his way to the ceremony in 2010, but was fourth to Auburn's Cam Newton.

"It's hard not to get emotional because it's been a long journey," Mariota said. "You're

feeling so excited, but at the same time you have to give thanks to everyone that's got you there. That's why I got emotional because all the hard work of other people. I just know those sacrifices weren't easy."

The question now becomes whether Mariota can help lead Oregon to another first — a national championship — in a few weeks, when

TOP RIGHT: Oregon coach Mark Helfrich was in New York along with others from the University of Oregon.
Thomas Boyd/The Oregonian/OregonLive

BOTTOM RIGHT: Heisman Trophy finalists Melvin Gordon of Wisconsin; Amari Cooper of Alabama; and Oregon's Marcus Mariota walk to the Best Buy Theater in New York City for Dec. 13's award ceremony.
Thomas Boyd/The Oregonian/OregonLive

the second-seeded Ducks (12-1) face third-seeded Florida State (13-0) in a College Football Playoff semifinal at the Rose Bowl on Jan. 1.

"To get an opportunity to be in a national championship, I would trade everything to be the eventual winner," Mariota said.

Mariota is the 35th quarterback and 17th junior to win the Heisman, and he has maintained he has yet to decide whether he will forgo his senior season and enter the NFL draft. But even he wouldn't deny it has been a nearly ideal season, as he led the nation in passing efficiency and became only the sixth player in Football Bowl Subdivision history with at least 9,000 career passing yards and 2,000 rushing yards.

Even head coach Mark Helfrich, who has attempted to deflect Heisman speculation the length of the 2014 season, admitted to feeling nearly overcome by the moment before Saturday's ceremony.

"We're flying into New York City (late Friday), and Marcus is on the cusp of history," said Helfrich, a native Oregonian who grew up a Ducks fan during the program's moribund era but now has the Ducks poised for history as a team, too.

Their relationship dates to 2010, when he traveled to Hawaii to scout an intriguing player who started only during his senior year at St. Louis High, a parochial powerhouse.

In Helfrich's recollection, it was Mariota's precision and power throwing one particular out-route that "perked me up a little bit."

"It was like a movie," Helfrich said.

Fitting, then, that Mariota's career at Oregon could end in such storybook fashion.

"Everything just comes together," Mullens said.

"It was a beautiful night." ∎

BELOW LEFT: Marcus Mariota's father, Toa, waits to see his son finish speaking during a press conference after winning the Heisman Trophy.
Thomas Boyd/The Oregonian/OregonLive

BELOW RIGHT: Marcus Mariota is presented several leis from his Hawaiian friends and family after winning the Heisman Trophy in New York City.
Thomas Boyd/The Oregonian/OregonLive

OPPOSITE: Having won the Heisman trophy the previous evening, Marcus Mariota enters the Ed Sullivan Theater to read David Letterman's Top Ten List before the Heisman Trophy gala later that night.
Thomas Boyd/The Oregonian/OregonLive

RIGHT: Heisman Trust president William J. Dockery hands the trophy to Marcus Mariota as he is officially inducted at the 80th Annual Heisman Trophy Dinner Gala at the Marquis Marriott in New York City. Thomas Boyd/The Oregonian/OregonLive

BELOW LEFT: An Oregon banner is displayed between banners for Florida State and Alabama at the Heisman gala in New York City.

Thomas Boyd/The Oregonian/OregonLive

BELOW RIGHT: An ice sculpture of the Heisman Trophy is on display during the gala event. Thomas Boyd/The Oregonian/OregonLive

OPPOSITE: Wearing leis bestowed upon him by friends and family, Mariota speaks at a news conference after winning the Heisman.

Thomas Boyd/The Oregonian/OregonLive

His attitude outshines his high aptitude

JASON QUICK
THE OREGONIAN/OREGONLIVE

While most around the nation looked at Marcus Mariota holding his Heisman Trophy on Saturday night and thought of his excellence on the football field, there was an entirely different reaction from his own team in Eugene.

For many on the Oregon Ducks, they thought not of plays that defined Mariota, but of actions.

They thought of a banana peel and a trash can more than his key shovel pass to Royce Freeman against Michigan State.

They thought of his 90-minute drive down Interstate 5 more than his somersaulting touchdown run against Wyoming.

And more than his toughness in absorbing seven sacks at Washington State, when he still completed 21 of 25 passes for 329 yards and five touchdowns, they remembered how quickly and how emphatically he changed the subject that day in the cafeteria.

"When I think about the Heisman Trophy, I think of excellence on and off the field," Oregon offensive coordinator Scott Frost said. "And I can't think of a more worthy recipient in my lifetime than Marcus Mariota."

So while the Downtown Athletic Club on Saturday immortalized Mariota's accomplishments on the field with this annual award given to college football's best player, a bigger message was being spread in Eugene.

Sometimes legacies are created off the field.

And it's those legacies that last long after the spirals and somersaulting touchdowns fade into history.

• • •

Hroniss Grasu couldn't remember the exact date, or the city, but the Oregon center still remembers the trash can. And the banana peel.

It was sometime last season, during one of the Ducks' road games, and the team was preparing to leave for the stadium from their hotel.

As the players nourished themselves, one of the Ducks discarded a banana peel into a wastebasket. When the peel landed, it rested on the rim, half in, half out. The impact of the tossed peel caused the already unhinged garbage liner to sag inside the can; leaving the peel still propped on the rim.

"So Marcus goes over there," Grasu said. "And he picks up the peel."

Amid the hustle and bustle of 50-plus football players preparing to board a bus, few watched Mariota. But Grasu, who forged a bond with Mariota over the last two seasons, eyed his friend.

"He didn't just pick up the peel," Grasu said. "He fixed the liner in the trash can, too. Made it right. He didn't have to do that. But that's Marcus, doing the right thing."

• • •

In our thirst to be captivated, we often turn to drama, or controversy.

And that's why many, including Mariota himself, find him boring.

He never stirred up the scintillating copy of some of his Heisman colleagues, but yet he became oddly captivating in his pureness.

He spurned the first chance to go to the NFL and make millions, instead opting to return to Oregon for his redshirt junior season to further his education and chase a goal with his "brothers" on the football team.

And while in Eugene, he capitalized the S in student-athlete.

In his first three years at Oregon, Mariota completed his requirements for a degree in general science, which calls for class loads that are anything but general. He wants to pursue a career in sports medicine, perhaps becoming a physical therapist, and apparently he's as good with his spiral notebook as he is tossing a spiral.

This month, he was named to the Pac-12 All-

Academic second team, no doubt a testament to study habits that rival his work ethic in the weight room and film sessions. Teammates say he often begged employees at the Jaqua Student Academic Center to stay open past closing time so he could continue studying.

Steve Stolp, the executive director of the Jaqua, said last year that Mariota was a regular in the academic center, even though his grade point average was high enough to excuse him from being required to be there. Stolp said Mariota would hole up in a corner of the center for privacy.

"I respect him immensely for the amount of work he puts in," Stolp said last year. "I've seen a lot of student-athletes over the years, and I have been here since 1998, but I haven't seen any — well, I should say very few — work as hard as he does. There have been a few, but none with the pressures that he has outside of school."

Beyond school, he has used his fame to help sick kids, and to pay tribute to fallen friends.

"It's hard to put into words just what kind of person he is," receiver Keanon Lowe said. "On the field, he's obviously brilliant. But off the field, he is one of the most genuine people I've met in my life. He's just a special guy."

• • •

The most difficult task presented to the Ducks this season may not have been Michigan State's defense, or the dual threat of UCLA quarterback Brett Hundley.

The biggest challenge might have been adequately describing the breadth and depth of Mariota.

He rarely, if ever, loses his composure, perhaps a byproduct of his Hawaiian heritage and the "Hang Loose" sign he waves to the crowd upon exiting the field.

But there was a time when he became angry at a teammate.

Two years ago, linebacker Tony Washington was returning from a trip home to Los Angeles when his car gave out about 100 miles south of Eugene. Parched and wheezing from leaking transmission fluid, Washington's car limped to the side of Interstate 5.

He called his roommate, Josh Huff. And Huff called Mariota.

About two hours later, there was Mariota, pulling up beside Washington with Huff and teammate Bronson Yim in tow. They had a container of transmission fluid for Washington's car, then followed him to a gas station where his car could be repaired.

"At the gas station, I went to give Marcus money, because it was like an hour and a half, two hours outside of Eugene," Washington said. "But he would not take the gas money."

Standing outside of Mariota's car, Washington

BELOW LEFT: Mariota talks to Oregon athletic director Rob Mullens on the dais before he is officially inducted at the 80th Annual Heisman Trophy Dinner Gala at the Marquis Marriott in New York City on Dec. 15.
Thomas Boyd/The Oregonian/OregonLive

BELOW RIGHT: Mariota, leaving the podium after being officially presented with the Heisman Trophy, is the second Heisman winner from the state of Oregon. Terry Baker of Oregon State won the Heisman in 1962.
Thomas Boyd/The Oregonian/OregonLive

kept insisting Mariota take the gas money. Mariota, still seated in the driver's seat, would not budge.

"Pretty soon, he started getting mad, because I kept offering it to him," Washington said. "So he started rolling up the window, even while I was talking to him."

Before the window reached the top, Washington wadded up his bills and threw it through the gap.

"Then I ran off before he could say anything," Washington said. "But, I don't know. It might sound like a small thing, but I think it just goes to show you who Marcus is."

Mariota makes an impression up and down the roster.

Walk-on receiver Austin Daich recalled to The Oregonian's John Canzano that, upon his arrival in Eugene, he was unsure of how he would be received as a walk-on at a powerhouse program such as Oregon. Mariota quickly put him at ease, inviting him to play golf.

So there was Daich: one moment worrying about his place on a team, and the next replacing divots with the greatest player in school history.

"Even all the great stories you hear about him, you still don't feel like they can explain how good a person he is," Daich told Canzano. "The Heisman thing, most guys would let that go to their heads."

• • •

The Heisman this season has probably been a bigger deal to Mariota's teammates than the quarterback himself.

One day this fall, as teammates sat around a table in the team's cafeteria, linebacker Derrick Malone remembers the conversation turning to the Heisman.

But one person at the table put an immediate end to the conversation: Mariota.

"He was having no part of it," Malone said.

The players wanted to talk about the Heisman candidates, and the developing race, and Mariota gave them a look that Malone described as "I don't really care."

"That's why I think he is so successful, because with him, it's all about the team," Malone said.

It is telling that the biggest blemish on Mariota's football resume is some anonymous scout famously proclaiming this season that Mariota may be "too nice" for the NFL.

"Like if you punched him in the stomach, he might apologize to you," the scout told Sports Illustrated.

Well, he got half of it right.

Mariota is nice.

He shows up on teammates' doorsteps at 1 a.m. when he hears they have had a bad day. Teammates say he is among the first to offer condolences when a parent or loved one passes away. And others say he insists on paying for lunch if he knows the person is running low on money.

"I have never in my life been around someone so kind," Malone said.

• • •

For the first time, the Heisman will rest in Eugene, adding further evidence of Oregon's ascension among college football royalty.

But hopefully, a greater lesson resonates from this award.

Yes, when Mariota has grayed and his playing days are behind him, the Heisman will assure his on-the-field accomplishments live on.

But hopefully, so too does his true essence.

Hopefully this award will help people remember the heart underneath his No. 8.

Hopefully people remember he was both a student and an athlete.

Hopefully, people will remember a player can be in a class by himself, and remain classy in the process.

For me, I won't forget a November afternoon leading up to the Colorado game.

It was a Tuesday, which for media means from 11:35 a.m. to 11:50, there's an opportunity to ask questions to Oregon coach Mark Helfrich in the press conference room inside the Hatfield-Dowlin Complex. From 11:50 to noon Mariota takes the seat behind the microphone.

As Helfrich spoke at the head table, Mariota was outside in the lobby, conducting a one-on-one interview with George Schroeder of USA Today. The session with Helfrich ended early, leaving the main press conference room silent with reporters.

When Mariota entered through the back, and noticed everyone waiting, he blanched.

"I apologize for keeping you guys waiting," he said as he hurried to the microphone.

It was 11:47 a.m. Technically he was three minutes early. Nobody was kept waiting.

The real wait will be the time before another player with the combination of Mariota's ability and character walks through those doors.

"He is a guy," Lowe said, "you are lucky to meet once in your lifetime." ∎

#2 OREGON 59, #3 FLORIDA STATE 20

'SOFT' DUCKS FIND FSU'S GLASS JAW

By Andrew Greif
The Oregonian/OregonLive

PASADENA, Calif. — Before they smashed a Rose Bowl record for points, before they celebrated with confetti snow angels and before they turned a hallowed venue into their own personal playground, the Oregon Ducks wandered into practice last spring and found a new addition: a black leather punching bag dangling from a stand.

Amid tackling dummies, sleds and cones, the Ducks had found the symbol for their season.

It served no obvious purpose, it seemed. Except that it explained everything, head coach Mark Helfrich would tell his team, about the mentality needed to achieve the ultimate goal. Before every practice, each Duck takes a swing.

"We punch in," Helfrich said. "But we don't punch out."

On Thursday afternoon at the Rose Bowl, the routine that began behind closed doors was on display for all the college football world to see. And it was a knockout.

The No. 2 Ducks overwhelmed No. 3 Florida State, 59-20, with a stunning mix of speed and power thanks to a 27-point third quarter that snapped the third-ranked Seminoles' 29-game winning streak in historic fashion, sending the Ducks to the national championship game for the second time in school history.

"We were talking before that you don't want to get overconfident, but I really felt if we executed like we were capable of, this thing wasn't going to be close," offensive line coach Steve Greatwood said. "It wasn't."

No one in the 101-year history of the storied bowl game had ever scored as many points or racked up as many yards (639) as the Ducks did

---

OPPOSITE: Running back Thomas Tyner plays in his first game since November 8. Tyner lead Oregon's rushing offense with 124 yards on 13 carries for two touchdowns, averaging 9.5 yards per carry.

Bruce Ely/The Oregonian/OregonLive

RIGHT: Marcus Mariota gathers with teammates in the tunnel before entering the stadium to face Florida State in the 101st Rose Bowl. Thomas Boyd/The Oregonian/OregonLive

en route to their second Rose Bowl win in four years and school record for victories.

The Seminoles entered with the mystique; after trailing six times at halftime this season, they kept finding ways to win behind 2013 Heisman Trophy winner Jameis Winston.

And they had the milestones — their streak was the nation's third-longest since 1970. All week, the Seminoles tried to dodge the perception that they were the villain in the matchup, stemming from several accusations of criminal behavior off the field. Yet they didn't exactly run away from the storyline that they were the bigger, badder team.

"We heard all week that Florida State was over there calling us soft and you guys saw the game," said receiver Darren Carrington, who caught touchdowns of 56 and 30 yards in a three-play span in the third quarter and finished with a career-high 165 yards on seven receptions.

"You should never want to give a team something to fuel off in the locker room. That just got our motors running."

It all evaporated in a rapid-fire hail of errors in the third quarter that turned a showcase into a shellacking. The Ducks forced five turnovers and scored 34 points from them, their defense's playmaking ability equal on this day to that of their much-publicized offense.

Fumbles by FSU running back Dalvin Cook set up both of Carrington's touchdowns, the first turnover forced by linebacker Derrick Malone's heady snatch of the ball from behind, and the second on a hit by safety Erick Dargan (who also nabbed his team-leading seventh interception).

"They couldn't recover," secondary coach John Neal said. "That's devastating, it's just devastating. ... That stuff gets in your head. So, it was just

really awesome."

The backbreaker play, and the one that sent the partisan Ducks crowd of 91,322 into mock chants of FSU's "Tomahawk Chop," was Winston's fumble on fourth-and-five while stumbling backward with 1:36 remaining in the third quarter.

As the ball fell out of his hands, it bounced perfectly into those of outside linebacker Tony Washington, who scooped and scored from 58 yards to take a 45-20 lead.

"That was a great run by our guys in terms of maintaining focus and finishing," said Helfrich, who's now 24-3 as head coach.

And the turnover figure doesn't include a three-play, goal-line stand that spanned the first and second quarters, the Seminoles unable to

score a TD from just 6 inches out. And it doesn't take into account that UO was doing this without several missing starters, including receiver Devon Allen, who didn't return after appearing to injure a knee on the opening kickoff.

In only the third meeting of Heisman winners ever, Winston finished 29-of-45 passing for 348 yards, a touchdown and an interception. Mariota was 26-of-36 passing for 338 yards with two touchdowns. But he staged a rope-a-dope second half, completing 8-of-10 passes while also running for a 23-yard touchdown.

The Ducks found their rhythm with a steady diet of passes to the sideline to widen the gaps between Florida State's seven All-Atlantic Coast defenders. Then they ran up the middle, mostly with Thomas Tyner (124 yards and a touchdown), or looked downfield to tight end Evan Baylis, an unexpected contributor whose six catches Thursday were more than his entire season's total (4) entering the game.

"We know what the perception is," running back Thomas Tyner said. "We know what it really is about and how we really play on the field. If you want to perceive us like that, it's OK."

OPPOSITE: Wide receiver Charles Nelson catches a pass in the first quarter. He had four receptions for 40 yards during the game. Thomas Boyd/The Oregonian/OregonLive

BELOW: Marcus Mariota tosses a shovel pass to Nelson. Thomas Boyd/The Oregonian/OregonLive

RIGHT: Nelson leaps for the end zone after taking a shovel pass from Mariota in the first quarter. Nelson landed just short of the end zone. Thomas Boyd/The Oregonian/OregonLive

It was Helfrich and Co. testing the soft spots of Florida State's inconsistent defense before launching its uppercuts.

"We just wanted to throw a ton of formations at them and try to create a little confusion and do it as fast as we could," said offensive coordinator Scott Frost. "The deal with that is you don't know where the breakdowns will happen but inevitably they're going to get misaligned and misfit something and we've got the guys that executed it well enough and a quarterback that can see it. And we made them pay for it."

When they retreated to their locker room, the Ducks passed around the silver Rose Bowl trophy and danced to The Notorious B.I.G's "Juicy," with its hook — "and if you don't know, now you know" — perhaps a message for those checking out the Ducks, and their supposedly too-finessed style, for the first time and wondering if they could hang with the 'Noles.

But they also kept a close eye on the televisions hanging from the ceiling, where Ohio State and Alabama played in the playoff's other semifinal.

The season isn't over yet.

"We're going to keep punching it," Frost said. "For another week and a half." ∎

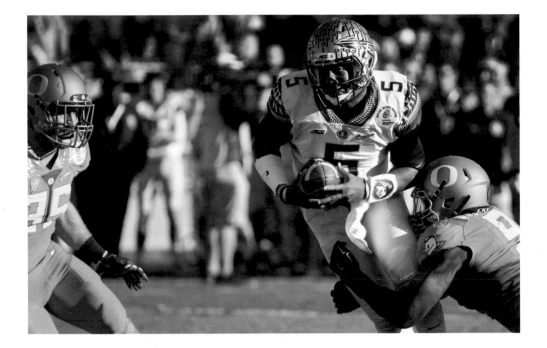

OPPOSITE: Royce Freeman scores Oregon's first touchdown at 6:55 in the first quarter, capping a 9-play, 73-yard drive. The two-point conversion put the Ducks ahead 8-3, giving them a lead they would never relinquish. Thomas Boyd/The Oregonian/OregonLive

LEFT: Linebacker Tony Washington stops Florida State's Jameis Winston from getting into the end zone on fourth down to open the second quarter. The Ducks took over possession at the 1-yard line and kept the ball for nearly five minutes, capping a 19-play drive of 88 yards with an Aidan Schneider 28-yard field goal. It was their longest drive of the day. Bruce Ely/The Oregonian/OregonLive

BELOW LEFT: Tight end Evan Baylis had six receptions for 73 yards, averaging 12.2 yards per reception during the game. Bruce Ely/The Oregonian/OregonLive

BELOW RIGHT: Mariota passes against Florida State in the second quarter. For the day Mariota was 26 of 36 for 338 yards, throwing two touchdowns and only his third interception of the season. Thomas Boyd/The Oregonian/OregonLive

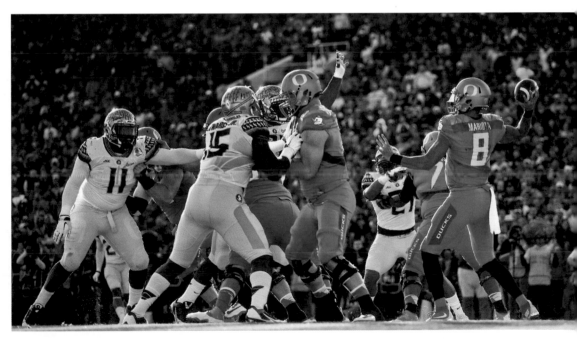

OPPOSITE TOP LEFT: Marcus Mariota joins teammates in the end zone after throwing a 30 yard touchdown to Darren Carrington at 4:21 in the third quarter. Bruce Ely/The Oregonian/OregonLive

OPPOSITE TOP MIDDLE: Mariota often had no one around him as he passed. Thomas Boyd/The Oregonian/OregonLive

OPPOSITE TOP RIGHT: Darren Carrington lead all receivers with seven receptions for 165 yards and two touchdowns. He averaged 23.6 yards per reception. Thomas Boyd/The Oregonian/OregonLive

OPPOSITE BOTTOM: Carrington hauls in a 56-yard pass for his first touchdown of the game at 6:43 in the third quarter. Thomas Boyd/The Oregonian/OregonLive

LEFT: Twilight fades as the Ducks begin the fourth quarter. On this play, Marcus Mariota would carry the ball into the end zone and the Ducks into the record book, scoring their 51st point of the game. The previous high score was 49 points, held twice by Michigan, and most recently by USC in 2008. Bruce Ely/The Oregonian/OregonLive

BELOW LEFT: Seminoles wide receiver Ermon Lane is stopped. Bruce Ely/The Oregonian/OregonLive

BELOW RIGHT: Coach Mark Helfrich joins his players on the field. Thomas Boyd/The Oregonian/OregonLive

ABOVE LEFT: The Rose Bowl was awash in green and yellow as fans were on hand to support their Ducks. Thomas Boyd/The Oregonian/OregonLive

ABOVE RIGHT: Jameis Winston tries to stop linebacker Tony Washington after Winston fumbled in the third quarter.
Bruce Ely/The Oregonian/OregonLive

RIGHT: Washington leads the charge after Winston's fumble. Thomas Boyd/The Oregonian/OregonLive

OPPOSITE: Washington runs 58 yards for a touchdown with 1:36 remaining in the third quarter. Thomas Boyd/The Oregonian/OregonLive

RIGHT: Offensive lineman Hroniss Grasu takes the trophy to the locker room after the celebration ends on the field. Grasu played his first game since being injured in the game against Utah on November 8.

Bruce Ely/The Oregonian/OregonLive

OPPOSITE: Running back Byron Marshall celebrates with a rose after beating Florida State 59-20.

Thomas Boyd/The Oregonian/OregonLive

BELOW LEFT: Mariota and Washington hold up the trophy after beating Florida State 59-20. They were named offensive and defensive players of the game.

Thomas Boyd/The Oregonian/OregonLive

BELOW RIGHT: Helfrich and Mariota talk on the trophy stand after beating Florida State 59-20.

Thomas Boyd/The Oregonian/OregonLive

A tale of two Heisman winners: 'We' dominates 'me'

JOHN CANZANO
THE OREGONIAN/OREGONLIVE

PASADENA, Calif. — The Rose Bowl staffers charged with staging the postgame news conference set out three black, stackable chairs on Thursday. The one on the far right drew the big assignment.

Florida State quarterback Jameis Winston occupied it first. He arrived late, wearing full uniform, minus his helmet. When Winston walked in, he leaned in to hug coach Jimbo Fisher, and as he craned toward his coach you couldn't miss the green grass stains streaking down the back of his jersey.

Oregon beat Florida State 59-20. The Ducks won physically. They won emotionally. The Ducks played better, they coached better, they dressed better. But here's what Winston said: "This game could have went either way, if you want to be — if everybody in this room just want to be real with themselves, this game could have went either way. We turned the ball over a lot. We beat ourself. Just be real with yourself right

now. We beat ourself."

By 39 points, in fact.

So it turns out this was some night for Florida State after all. Winston beat Winston. The Seminoles beat the Seminoles. The only surprise is that Winston didn't run to the rose bushes just outside the interview tent, snap off a big blooming red one and clench it in his teeth while he stood in the loser's circle twisting and rationalizing what amounted to a first-rate beat down.

"Tonight was unfortunate," Winston said. "It wasn't just they were stopping us. Their offense did great. Their defense was great. But we were never stopped at all."

I suppose that's what a team that won 29 consecutive games says when it gets boat-raced in No. 30. Also, what the leader of a team that mostly walked off the Rose Bowl field without shaking

the hands of Oregon's players says. Winston sat straight-faced in that stackable chair, piling up the

---

ABOVE: Linebacker Rodney Hardrick puts pressure on Florida State's Jameis Winston, forcing him to scramble from the pocket and eventually fumble the ball, which was recovered by Tony Washington for a 58 yard touchdown. Thomas Boyd/The Oregonian/OregonLive

OPPOSITE: Facing 4th and 2 at Florida State's 23-yard line, Marcus Mariota kept the ball and ran for his lone rushing touchdown of the day. After the conversion the Ducks lead 52-20. This play broke the Rose Bowl record for most points scored by one team, marking the first time a team has scored more than 49 points. Thomas Boyd/The Oregonian/OregonLive

nonsense, finishing his statement with the word "honest" as if that would make it true.

"It was never over," he said. "Honestly, it was never over. We just got beat, turned the ball over too many times. But it still ain't over. We can go play again, honest."

Winston is no chump. He's the 2013 Heisman Trophy winner. A guy who smiles through chaos. A big-game hunter who has Auburn's prized head on his apartment wall from last season's national title game.

Oregon chased that guy all over the Rose Bowl. The Ducks squeezed him and pressed him until Winston voluntarily flipped himself on his own can and fumbled the ball backwards in a fourth-down, reverse-somersault gymnastics move best described as the "Lasorda Tumble." (See: 2001 MLB All-Star Game.)

"Just — it was just an unfortunate play, man," Winston said. "I never thought that I would slip, throw the ball backwards. Man, it's just — it's a very unfortunate play, but that's football."

Keep that chair in mind. Because when Winston was through with it, he didn't bother to push it in. He just stood, then walked off, presumably toward Florida State's victory party.

Ducks quarterback Marcus Mariota slid into the chair next. Same spot. Same seat. Same microphone, right side. In fact, the thing might have even still been warm from Winston taking the first-ever, recorded sitting victory lap in it. But what ensued with Mariota was a revealing exercise in humility.

Mariota said this whole Rose Bowl thing was an incredible gift in a magical season and that Florida State was a worthy opponent. Also, when he was asked about the comparisons between himself and Winston, Mariota cringed.

"I was just happy for our team," he said. "The entire week, I really didn't want to focus on the matchup. I think that was just stuff that other people really wanted to talk about.

"I just wanted to focus on this team and for us to kind of go out there and be successful. It was just a great feeling and I'm happy for us."

Us.

Our team.

We.

These themes come up over and over around Oregon's players. In victory, and defeat. In good moments and disappointing ones.

In fact, Ducks coach Mark Helfrich said minutes earlier, "The most important part of understanding what we're all about is — it's we."

In theory, he's right. Smack. Dead. Between-the-eyes. Right. But anyone who has ever seen the Ducks play understands that this "we" mechanism is operated by the guy wearing the hard hat and the No. 8 jersey.

Mariota threw for 338 yards and two touch-downs. He rushed for 62 yards and another touchdown. When he missed throws, and he insisted there were a few bad ones in the first half, or when he threw an interception (and he did in this game), there was no deflection, no excuses, no rationalization. Just Mariota, calm and poised, coming back to make another play.

It's going to be suggested in the wake of Oregon's whipping of Florida State that Winston was the victim of karma. As if the gods of football sought justice. The point may be raised that he's flirted with disaster, on and off the field, for two seasons and went to sleep at night unscathed until Thursday night. But doing so would only continue the lazy narrative that Winston was busy spinning.

Florida State got beat. It got embarrassed. The Seminoles' final seven offensive drives of the Rose Bowl went like this: fumble, fumble, interception, fumble, punt, punt, punt.

The Ducks scored touchdowns on six consecutive possessions to start the second half and posted more points (59) than any team in any of the previous 100 Rose Bowls.

Florida State coach Jimbo Fisher, a few chairs down from Winston, said, "Once it got up to 45, it pressed us, and we really started pressing and making — and didn't let the ball stay in our hands and turned it over."

Oregon caused that. The Ducks did that. They realize that, right? Right?? The UO offense put such incredible pressure on Florida State that Winston tried to make impossible plays that imploded in his face. The Ducks' defense stripped the ball. It tackled. It made huge plays. It forced field goals and turnovers. And Mariota at some point, almost reluctantly, took over the game one methodical play after another and demonstrated why he's the greatest quarterback in college football.

This whole Winston vs. Mariota battle ended with a knockout. Not just on the field, but in the postgame news conference with both players occupying the same chair.

Winston's crowing act and Mariota's shrugging performance in one place, minutes apart. The acts couldn't have been more different. The feeling in the room couldn't have been more divergent. With apologies to Mariota, who wouldn't want any part of this comparison, the difference between the Heisman winners was never more apparent.

Winston and Mariota didn't just lead their teams in different directions Thursday. They cut the postgame news conference in two pieces, one of them a steaming pile of denial and the other a gleaming stack of leadership. That they walked out the same exit was a mere coincidence.

Mariota's Heisman speech goes down as the single greatest sports moment of 2014 in the state of Oregon. He probably owes a debt of gratitude not just to his parents, coaches and teammates, but a small assist to Winston, who undeniably figured in the minds of voters who were looking to cast a vote for a great player they knew would never embarrass the Heisman Trust.

Mariota is the correction from Winston, and some others. That they ended up on the same field on the same night, playing for the same title-game berth was poetry. At one juncture in the second half, Mariota was standing emotionless on the Ducks' sideline waiting for a kickoff while Winston was heated and jawing with his coach on the other side.

"Yes, but he always gets animated like that when he talks," Fisher said of Winston. "He does it when he's playing good. That's just his nature."

Lip readers know better.

Oregon is now focused on Arlington, Texas, and a date at Jerryworld. The Seminoles, meanwhile, appear to be rationalizing the notion that they're going back to Tallahassee empty-handed, clinging to the title of "Paper Champions."

The Seminoles were undefeated. They were the defending national champions. They had Winston. This wasn't supposed to happen. But I think the 101st Rose Bowl can best be summed up not with a statement, but with a simple question, one you knew the answer to when you saw Florida State evacuate the field so quickly after the game.

Which team would have wanted to play another quarter?

Just be real with yourself right now. ■

ABOVE: The Leishman trophy, designed by Tiffany & Co., is nearly 21-inches-tall, rendered in sterling silver, and requires nearly 16 pounds of sterling. The craftsmen need nearly three months to create each one.
Thomas Boyd/The Oregonian/OregonLive

OPPOSITE: Mariota hugs Winston after the game.
Thomas Boyd/The Oregonian/OregonLive

#4 OHIO STATE 42, #2 OREGON 20

AND IT ALL CAME DOWN TO THIS

By Andrew Greif
The Oregonian/OregonLive

ARLINGTON, Texas — The season's final play began as they all seemed to do in this most charmed year to be an Oregon Duck.

Four yards behind center, Marcus Mariota received the snap and dodged two tacklers with a ballerina's grace, pirouetting into open space and possibility.

Mariota squared his shoulders, lofted a pass 40 yards into the dome of AT&T Stadium and let it rip. How many plays looked this bad to start before, and how many times did they get added to his highlight reel afterward, anyway?

But it was all window dressing on a night long since decided against their favor.

OPPOSITE: The Oregon Ducks play Ohio State in the College Football Playoff National Championship at AT&T Stadium in Arlington, Texas. AT&T Stadium seats 80,000 and can hold 105,000 people, including standing room. The two center hung 1080p video monitors are each 160-feet wide and 72-feet tall, and weigh 1.2 million pounds each. Bruce Ely/The Oregonian/OregonLive

RIGHT: Injured Oregon Duck Ifo Ekpre-Olomu makes his way to the field prior to the game. Olomu was injured in practice after the regular season and missed the Rose Bowl and National Championship game.

Thomas Boyd/The Oregonian/OregonLive

Well before Mariota jogged back out on one last series, stadium workers in black pullovers positioned confetti cannons behind each sideline. All the final pass did, once it was intercepted by Ohio State's Eli Apple, was make it official: The first College Football Playoff ended with second-ranked Oregon seeing scarlet red, beaten 42-20 by a fourth-ranked Ohio State team that staged a master class in how to own a moment.

"This team," Ohio State coach Urban Meyer said, "wasn't supposed to do this."

Oregon was.

Stocked with a roster brimming with talent and a reservoir of resiliency, the Ducks possessed a MacGyver-like knack for digging themselves out of holes and emerging with hope — or at least a first down. They entered Monday with six missing starters but nine straight wins.

RIGHT: Puddles joins the Oregon Ducks cheer squad to entertain fans before the game.

Thomas Boyd/The Oregonian/OregonLive

BELOW LEFT: The Oregon Ducks take the field.

Bruce Ely/The Oregonian/OregonLive

BELOW RIGHT: Former Oregon coaches Mike Bellotti (left), Chip Kelly and Nick Aliotti on hand for the game.

Bruce Ely/The Oregonian/OregonLive

Down 21-10 at halftime, few blinked.

And when Danny Mattingly intercepted Ohio State quarterback Cardale Jones in the third quarter, and Oregon scored on the very next play on a 70-yard touchdown reception between Mariota and Byron Marshall, few were surprised. The Ducks forced a fumble on the next possession and kicked a field goal to cut the deficit to one, and the chase was on.

Four times the Ducks trailed at halftime this season, and three times they came back to win. Like Mariota, they made wriggling out of the impossible an art in 2014.

But two hours later, they trudged off the field under golden streamers shot 100 feet high because that precedent meant little against Ohio State (14-1). For not once this season had the Ducks (13-2) faced a back like Ezekiel Elliott, the Buckeye who rushed for a championship record 246 yards and four touchdowns and smushed the Ducks' title hopes in a bruising second half.

"It's unfortunate and a little bit insulting in a lot of ways that whoever loses this game, the word failure comes up as a descriptive for the season," said head coach Mark Helfrich, now 24-4 in two seasons. "As I told the guys in the locker room, that will never exist in these guys' vocabulary. Every player to a T has just battled and gutted this out."

After capitalizing on Ohio State's own mistakes and four turnovers — Jones was intercepted once, and fumbled twice — to keep itself in the game, it was Oregon's own errors that ultimately ended the season many will remember with a night the Ducks cannot wait to forget. They were 2-of-12 on third down and 0-of-2 on fourth down, including being stuffed on a goal-line stand when a handoff to Thomas Tyner was 1 yard short of the end zone.

Twice in the first quarter, critical drops by Charles Nelson and Dwayne Stanford put

---

ABOVE LEFT: Marcus Mariota passes on the first drive of the game. Thomas Boyd/The Oregonian/OregonLive

ABOVE RIGHT: Marcus Mariota's ability to scramble allows him to create space from defenders, giving him time to find a receiver. Bruce Ely/The Oregonian/OregonLive

ABOVE: Keanon Lowe celebrates his seven-yard touchdown reception for the first score of the game. Thomas Boyd/The Oregonian/OregonLive

OPPOSITE TOP AND BOTTOM: With Ohio State ahead 14-7 and moving the ball into Oregon territory to open the second quarter, Cardale Jones' fumble was recovered by Oregon's Alex Balducci. Bruce Ely and Thomas Boyd/The Oregonian/OregonLive

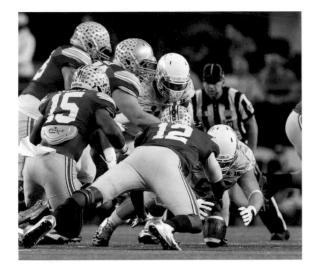

airbrakes on Oregon's runaway tempo.

The Ducks also committed 10 penalties and punted four times in the first quarter, their most in the opening 15 minutes since 2009. Starting for the first time since Sept. 13, Thomas Tyner rushed for 62 yards. Marshall hauled in a game-high 169 yards. But it wasn't enough. The Ducks are 0-9 all-time against Ohio State and 0-4 under Helfrich when scoring fewer than 30 points.

"Wanting to put the right finishing touch on it and that not happening is gutting to me, for them," Helfrich said. "But yeah, this was an unbelievable journey."

It's even more so an incredible achievement

for Ohio State, which won despite leaning on a third-string quarterback many thought was too immature to capitalize on the gifts of his prodigiously strong arm and huge, 6-foot-5, 250-pound frame, for the past three games. But for all of his costly turnovers, Jones was a force the Ducks rarely could pin down as Ohio State roared back for 21 unanswered points en route to the title.

On third-and-three in the third quarter, he ran over 300-pound nose tackle Alex Balducci for the first down on a drive that gave the Buckeyes a 28-20 lead. Meanwhile Mariota, his Heisman counterpart, passed for 333 yards and two touchdowns and became the first Pac-12 player

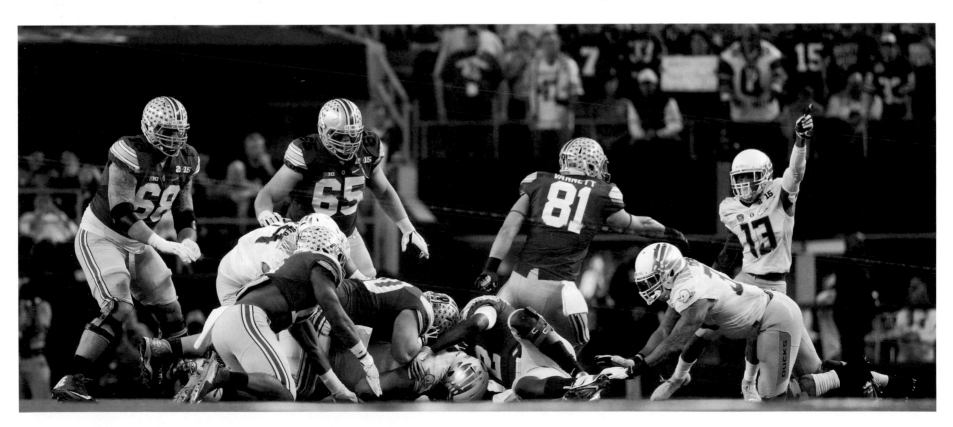

ever to rack up 5,000 yards of offense in a single season. If this was his final game in an Oregon uniform, he ended it with a passing touchdown in all 41 of his games.

But he was never quite able to manufacture the explosive plays that pushed him, and the Ducks, to college football's forefront this season. The senior class that began its career with a loss in a national championship game bookended it with heartbreak once again.

"I'm just sorry we came up a little short," Mariota said.

There remains a sliver of possibility that he will return for his senior season. The deadline for underclassmen to declare for the draft is Thursday. Afterward, Mariota spoke of possibly entering graduate school, and getting better with a team that will have the pieces to get back to another playoff.

But they won't get back Monday evening. ■

OPPOSITE BOTTOM LEFT: Byron Marshall signals a first down after a 20-yard completion from Marcus Mariota brought the Ducks to Ohio State's 28-yard line early in the second quarter. Bruce Ely/The Oregonian/OregonLive

OPPOSITE TOP RIGHT: Marcus Mariota (8) hands off to Thomas Tyner (24) on a 4th-and-goal attempt in the second quarter. Tyner was stopped inches short of the goal line. Bruce Ely/The Oregonian/OregonLive

OPPOSITE BOTTOM RIGHT: Thomas Tyner can't get the ball into the end zone on fourth down. Bruce Ely/The Oregonian/OregonLive

TOP LEFT: Behind 21-7 in the second quarter, Marcus Mariota looks to move the offense. Bruce Ely/The Oregonian/OregonLive

TOP RIGHT: Head coach Mark Helfrich talks with the officials after a personal foul was called on Ohio State's Michael Bennett. Thomas Boyd/The Oregonian/OregonLive

LEFT: Ducks wide receiver Dwayne Stanford hauls in a 28-yard reception into Buckeye territory during the second quarter. Thomas Boyd/The Oregonian/OregonLive

OPPOSITE: Byron Marshall runs with a 15-yard reception during the second quarter.

Thomas Boyd/The Oregonian/OregonLive

LEFT: With Eli Apple in pursuit, Marcus Mariota tries to turn the corner and runs out of bounds on the Ohio State 29-yard line.

Bruce Ely/The Oregonian/OregonLive

BELOW LEFT: Royce Freeman looks for running room in the red zone late in the second quarter.

Thomas Boyd/The Oregonian/OregonLive

BELOW RIGHT: Thomas Tyner heads to the locker room after the first half. Returning in the Rose Bowl after having missed several games due to injury, Tyner looks to be one of the bright spots in 2015.

Bruce Ely/The Oregonian/OregonLive

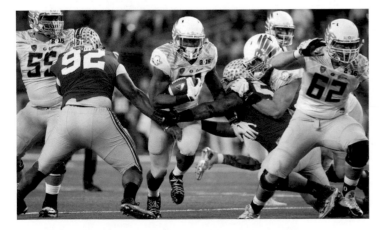

OPPOSITE TOP: Ducks linebacker Joe Walker (35) celebrates after Danny Mattingly intercepted a bobbled catch by Jalin Marshall on the Oregon 30-yard line early in the third quarter.

Thomas Boyd/The Oregonian/OregonLive

OPPOSITE BOTTOM LEFT, MIDDLE AND RIGHT: Byron Marshall hauls in a 70-yard touchdown reception to open the third quarter, bringing the score to 21-17.

Bruce Ely and Thomas Boyd/The Oregonian/OregonLive

ABOVE LEFT: Byron Marshall drops the ball in the end zone after a 70-yard touchdown reception from Marcus Mariota early in the third quarter, making the score 21-17. It would be the last touchdown of the Ducks' season. Thomas Boyd/The Oregonian/OregonLive

BELOW LEFT: Marcus Mariota (8) is congratulated by lineman Tyrell Crosby (73) and lineman Jake Fisher (75) after throwing a 70-yard touchdown to Byron Marshall early in the third quarter.

Bruce Ely/The Oregonian/OregonLive

RIGHT: The Ducks defense celebrates a one-yard loss by Ohio State quarterback Cardale Jones in the third quarter. Thomas Boyd/The Oregonian/OregonLive

BELOW LEFT AND MIDDLE: Reminiscent of Jameis Winston's fumble in the Rose Bowl two weeks earlier, Cardale Jones fumbles while scrambling away from linebacker Tyson Coleman (33). Thomas Boyd and Bruce Ely/The Oregonian/OregonLive

BELOW RIGHT: The Oregon Ducks bring down Ezekiel Elliott after a short gain in the third quarter.
Bruce Ely/The Oregonian/OregonLive

OPPOSITE: Ohio State running back Ezekiel Elliott runs during the third quarter. He scored four touchdowns and rushed for 246 yards, 114 more yards than the Ducks team combined. Bruce Ely/The Oregonian/OregonLive

ABOVE: Oregon fans react as the Ducks fall behind and run out of time.
Thomas Boyd/The Oregonian/OregonLive

ABOVE LEFT: Marcus Mariota walks off the field after a heavy tackle by Joey Bosa.
Bruce Ely/The Oregonian/OregonLive

LEFT: Marcus Mariota runs from the pursuit of Adolphus Washington.
Thomas Boyd/The Oregonian/OregonLive

FAR LEFT: Facing third down with four yards to go, Marcus Mariota attempts a pass to Evan Baylis, which was broken up by Eli Apple. The Ducks settled for a 23-yard field goal by Aidan Schneider with 8:21 gone in the third quarter. The field goal made the score 21-20, but it would be the last points of the Ducks' season.
Bruce Ely/The Oregonian/OregonLive

ABOVE: Nick Aliotti consoles an Oregon player after the Ducks loss to Ohio State.
Bruce Ely/The Oregonian/OregonLive

ABOVE RIGHT: Hroniss Grasu and Jeff Lockie are consoled by former Oregon defensive coordinator Nick Aliotti (obscured) as they leave the field after the game.
Bruce Ely/The Oregonian/OregonLive

RIGHT: Marcus Mariota walks off the field as confetti rains during the celebration of Ohio State's victory.
Bruce Ely/The Oregonian/OregonLive

FAR RIGHT: The Oregon Ducks walk off the field after losing to Ohio State in the College Football Playoff National Championship.
Bruce Ely/The Oregonian/OregonLive

Is Mariota content to go out this way?

John Canzano
The Oregonian/OregonLive

ARLINGTON, Texas — If there was ever a reason. If there ever existed an argument. If there was ever a chance that Marcus Mariota might pause before cleaning out his college locker, before saying goodbye to Eugene for good, before declaring for the NFL draft.

Monday would be part of it.

Ohio State loaded up the Mack Truck known as running back Ezekiel Elliott in the title game. They flipped on the CB radio. They gassed up at a truck stop. Then the Buckeyes stepped on the pedal and rode Elliott to the national championship, flattening the Ducks 42-20.

Elliott could not be tackled. He could not be stopped. Ohio State coach Urban Meyer even piled an Elliott touchdown on in the final minute, flooring the gas pedal of his rig when he could have coasted home, presumably just in case TCU was watching.

But it was Mariota I was left thinking about, even as he scrambled around on that final play of his junior season, spinning out of the pocket, desperate and searching for a 22-point play as time expired.

Mariota threw into triple coverage. The ball was intercepted. The game ended. Confetti fell. And I wondered, does the Heisman Trophy winner want to go out like that while he still has one season of eligibility?

In the postgame Mariota was asked if he's decided on turning pro. He said, "I have not. I'll talk with my family over the next few days and make a decision."

Hold that thought.

The Ducks quarterback completed 24 of 37 passes for 333 yards, two touchdowns and that interception against Ohio State. His junior season: 42 touchdowns, four interceptions. And though he might very well march off toward a professional career I wonder if maybe Mariota feels there's unfinished business here.

Will he do what Chip Kelly ultimately could not? Will he do what any other college football

ABOVE: Marcus Mariota is pursued by Michael Bennett in the second quarter. Bruce Ely/The Oregonian/OregonLive

player in America would not? Will Mariota enroll in a postgraduate program and tell the 27 other juniors on this Oregon roster that he's coming back for another season?

Unthinkable, right? Impossible, right? Absurd, I'd be the first to say. Yet I find myself typing this sentence: If Mariota comes back for another season, the Ducks will get back here.

I'd agree that this debate is a nonstarter for any other can't-miss NFL first-round draft pick. But anyone who has ever talked with Mariota or watched him compete understands that he's an exotic person. He's not like anyone else.

"It hurts," Mariota said after the game. "You put so much work and so much effort into the year. It's tough to go out with a loss."

After a loss to Stanford his sophomore season he cried, then came back this season and stuck a stake in the heart of the Cardinal. After a loss to Arizona earlier this season he stayed up all night watching film on his iPad in his parents' hotel room, then came back and drilled the Wildcats

in the conference title game. If he's interested, if he's still hungry, if he's driven at all by the possibilities, I'd argue that Ohio State made a strong case for Mariota to return for a senior season.

Mark Helfrich said, "This was an unbelievable journey."

What if it's not over? A national title is still out there. A second Heisman is still out there for Mariota. A lot of his teammates are still coming back.

Legacy isn't important to Mariota. The relationships are. He never once said he wanted to be a Heisman Trophy winner before he held the trophy in his hands. He called the Rose Bowl victory and the Pac-12 title, his highlights this season, team accomplishments. The ultimate team accomplishment, a national championship, eluded the Ducks on Monday.

Mariota said of whether the loss would bring him back for another season: "There's a lot of other things that have to play into that decision, starting grad school, having another year to improve, there are a lot of other things that could bring me back, not just this loss."

The question on this playoff stretch for the Ducks has centered, all along, on the idea that Oregon would be lost without Mariota next season. They'd have to run the ball with Thomas Tyner and Royce Freeman. They'd dissolve without Mariota from a championship contender

---

LEFT: Marcus Mariota wears a lei and faces the media in the locker room after the game. Within 48 hours he would announce that he would file paperwork to declare for the NFL draft, forgoing his senior season of eligibility.
Bruce Ely/The Oregonian/OregonLive

into a three-loss outfit with no punching power.

It's been said that you have to sniff around a title before you can win one. The pain of a near miss is a motivator. It burns. It stings. It makes a competitor seethe. I've seen Mariota fail, but never walk away after.

The Ducks couldn't tackle on Monday night. They failed to capitalize on four Ohio State turnovers, getting only 10 points off them. Oregon was uncharacteristically sloppy, dropping a couple of key passes early, missing holes, committing penalties.

You play this game 10 times and Ohio State wins nine of them.

But if you gave Oregon the gift of Mariota's senior season, stacked it with the returning starters, glazed it with the burn the Ducks felt as they left the field watching Ohio State celebrate, you might just have something.

Helfrich compared Mariota to Dan Marino after the game. Also his fame to Madonna and Cher. With the quarterback sitting beside him, Helfrich said, "There has never been one greater — none."

After the game, Ducks players, coaches and fans walked around hugging one another. The outfit needs a hug today. The return of Mariota would be the equivalent.

The NFL is a meat grinder. There are few happy endings. Locker rooms are office parks. Relationships are shallow. Teammates come and go. Mariota has always struck me as the kind of person who understands that college is the greatest time of his life.

Does he want 12 more months of this?

We'll know in a few days.

But if he does, Oregon must then figure out is how to tackle a Mack Truck. ∎

ACKNOWLEDGEMENTS

OREGONLIVE
The Oregonian

Produced by
The Oregonian/OregonLive

Mark Katches, editor and vice president
of content

Hallie Janssen, vice president of
marketing and digital solutions

Ben Sherman, director of sports
and multimedia

Therese Bottomly, director of state
content

Joel Odom, managing producer/sports

Mike Zacchino, manager/multimedia

Authors **Andrew Greif, Tyson Alger,
John Canzano, Jason Quick and
Ken Goe**

Photographers **Bruce Ely, Thomas Boyd,
Randy L. Rasmussen and Michael Lloyd**

Copy editors **Jim Hays, Mike Zacchino
and Jacob Arnold**

AUTHORS

Andrew Greif   **Tyson Alger**   **John Canzano**   **Jason Quick**   **Ken Goe**

PHOTOGRAPHERS

Bruce Ely   **Thomas Boyd**   **Randy L. Rasmussen**   **Michael Lloyd**